The

Anticipated

Christ

A Journey Through Advent and Christmas

By Brian Zahnd

The Anticipated Christ
A Journey Through Advent and Christmas

Copyright 2022 by Brian Zahnd
www.brianzahnd.com

Published by Spello Press

ISBN: 978-0-9668421-2-8

For Jude, Finn, Evey, Liam,
Mercy, Hope, Pax, and Honor.

Introduction to
The Anticipated Christ

Ours is a secular age. The sacred is pushed to the periphery. To keep the sacred at the center of our lives is a heroic act of defiance. To be a religious person in an irreligious world may be the last act of rebellion. I advocate such rebellion. I reject the trite aphorism, "I'm spiritual, but not religious." Of course, I'm spiritual, we all are, but I'm also religious—or at least I seek to be. Amorphous spirituality too easily becomes little more than a mood with a sprinkling of "wellness" techniques. I need something more rigorous, something more deeply rooted, something that draws upon the deep wells of ancient wisdom and practice. This is what we find in the Great Tradition of the Christian faith.

Part of what we find in the Great Tradition is a sacred calendar—a way of marking time through the course of the year by telling the gospel story of Jesus Christ. We have a secular calendar to coordinate our lives within a secular age, and we have a sacred calendar to form our lives through the gospel story. And, yes, a couple of holy days from the sacred calendar are firmly entrenched in the secular calendar—Christmas and Easter. But the way the sacred calendar and the secular calendar approach these holy days is quite different. In the Christian calendar Christmas is anticipated by four weeks of waiting. This is Advent—a word derived from a Latin word meaning "arrival." During Advent we await the arrival of the Messiah of whom the Hebrew prophets spoke. During Advent we allow the messianic poems of the Hebrew prophets to seep deeply into our soul. With Isaiah and the great company of Hebrew prophets we wait for the one who will bruise the serpent's head. We wait for Immanuel—the one who is God with us. We wait for the ruler to arise in Bethlehem who will shepherd God's people. We wait for the child born unto us upon whose shoulders the government will rest; we wait for the Prince of Peace in whose kingdom the lion lays down with the lamb. Advent is about waiting—a practice most of us in our secular age struggle with, but a holy practice we would be wise to cultivate.

During Advent we also visit the New Testament stories that precede the birth in Bethlehem. Stories like Zechariah and Gabriel in the Temple, the meeting of Mary and Elizabeth, the Annunciation, the Magnificat, and the birth of John the Baptist. All these prophecies and stories set the stage for Christmas to arrive with full force. And when Christmas does arrive, it's not a one-day celebration—the birth of Messiah is far too big an event to celebrate for a mere day. No, Christmas is a twelve-day feast during which we meditate on all the marvelous stories surrounding the birth of Jesus Christ that help us explore the meaning of the Incarnation. And after the twelve days of Christmas have run their course, we arrive at Epiphany where we celebrate and contemplate the revelation of Christ to the Gentiles, as the Magi come with their gifts to pay homage to the child born King of the Jews. This is what the six-week journey from the first Sunday in Advent to Epiphany is about. It's a journey out of secular banality and into the sacred mystery of the Incarnation.

I encourage you to read The Anticipated Christ as it is intended—don't fly through it in a day or two. Instead, read each meditation on the indicated day and read it slowly. The demand of the secular "Christmas Season" is to be in a great hurry, but the aim of Advent is to instill a quiet slowness into our soul. Each day's meditation begins with a brief reading from Scripture, followed by a three-page reflection, and concludes with a one or two sentence prayer. It doesn't take much time to read each day's selection, the challenge is to read it slowly. You can probably speed through it in three minutes but see if you can find a way to spend ten minutes with it. The richness will be revealed in the slowness. During Advent try to feel Israel's centuries-long wait for the promised Messiah. Let the anticipation build. And when we reach Christmas, don't take down the tree and pack away the decorations on December 26—the party has just begun! Join with the angels and the shepherds and the wisemen and Simeon and Anna and all the rest in the unbounded joy that comes with the birth of Christ.

> May the God of hope fill you with all joy and peace in believing, so that you may abound in hope by the power of the Holy Spirit. (Romans 15:13)

FIRST WEEK OF ADVENT
SUNDAY

Genesis 3:15
The Proto Gospel

The Bible tells a *big* story. Holy Scripture is a sacred saga of more than a thousand pages that takes us from creation to new creation, from paradise lost to paradise regained, from the Garden of Eden to the garden city of New Jerusalem. In every epic drama there are antagonists who threaten goodness and menace justice. In Tolkien's *The Lord of the Rings*, Sauron, Saruman, Gollum, Wormtongue, and a host of other villains imperil Middle Earth. In the Bible we find the likes of Pharaoh, Goliath, Nebuchadnezzar, King Herod, and Pontius Pilate among the villains who are in league with the very embodiment of evil itself—the devil. It's with these enemies that the heroes of the Bible—Moses, David, Daniel, John the Baptist, and most of all Jesus—must struggle and prevail. The Bible is not really an encyclopedia of God-facts or a journal of divine jurisprudence, it is primarily the epic story of God's ultimate triumph over evil. Admittedly there are moments in, say, Leviticus or Numbers, where the plot seems lost, but it's always found again and the Great Struggle continues.

The main antagonist in the Bible story first appears in the third chapter of Genesis. After two creation accounts where everything is declared "very good," a cunning serpent enters the story. We're not told who the serpent is or where it came from—it just appears. (The Bible offers almost no account of the origin of evil.) The serpent gives humanity deceitful advice that leads to a catastrophic exile from paradise and ultimately from life itself. Only much later, toward the end of the New Testament, is the deceitful serpent in Eden identified as the devil. The point of the story is that evil has arrived and now must be contended with. The drama of the biblical story has begun.

The story tells us that the Creator enters Eden to pronounce judgment. From now on, human life will endure painful labor and fruitless toil and will end with an inevitable return to the dust. Every human story will come to an end at a grave. The chapter concludes with Adam and Eve exiled from paradise. Only three chapters into the

Great Story tragedy has arrived. But in the judgment the Creator pronounces upon the serpent, there is a faint glimmer of hope. Someday the Seed of the woman will crush the head of the serpent. We don't know who the Seed is or when he will arrive or how he will prevail, but the story does foreshadow a hero who, though wounded in the process, will bring to its demise the origin of evil. Christian theology calls this foreshadowing the *protoevangelium*—the proto gospel or the first good news. As Adam and Eve are subjected to death and exiled from Eden, there is the foreshadowed hope that someday a man born of woman will triumph over sin and death. This is the messianic hope. This is the anticipated Christ.

Creator God, as we enter the season of Advent, may our hearts cultivate the blessed hope that your goodness, O God, is infinite and eternal, while evil and death are but finite and temporal. May we hold to the gospel hope that in the triumph of the Seed of the Woman, evil and death meet their demise. Amen.

First Week of Advent
Monday

Isaiah 2:1–5
In Days to Come

Yesterday we looked at the protoevangelium in Genesis as the first anticipation of Christ. Now we've jumped all the way to Isaiah. We already have a lot of the Big Story in our rearview mirror—Noah and the Flood, Abraham and the Patriarchs, Moses and the Exodus, David and the Kingdom of Israel are all behind us. For the next seventeen days we will be in Isaiah—first with Isaiah of Jerusalem and then with Isaiah of the Exile.

The Hebrew prophets were poets of profound imagination and are most responsible for shaping messianic expectations. The medium of the Hebrew prophets is poetry, not prose. Prose cannot approach the ineffable—only poetry is capable of this. It's through the poems of the Hebrew prophets that we begin to glimpse the contours of messianic anticipation. And these prophetic contours are never sharper than they are in

Isaiah—so much so that we may be tempted to speak of Isaiah as the Fifth Gospel.

Seven centuries before Christ, Isaiah of Jerusalem began a poem with these words: In days to come. He doesn't know when and even less how, but inspired by the Spirit, Isaiah imagines the kingdom of Israel becoming the true kingdom of Yahweh and gaining ascendency over the nations. This kingdom—let's call it the kingdom of God—will become famous the world over for its wisdom. A king will come to Jerusalem who possesses the very wisdom of Yahweh, and he will teach the way of God to the nations. And what will he teach? He will teach the way of peace. Those who hear and heed the wisdom of Yahweh will abandon the folly of war— for what greater madness is there than war? With war abandoned in response to the teaching of the wise king, weapons of war are converted into instruments of agriculture. Cain will never again accost Abel on a battlefield—fields are forever given to crops and herds, never again to slaughter and bloodshed.

When the first Christians read Isaiah's swords to plowshares poem, they recognized the wise king as Jesus and realized that God's kingdom of peace had been inaugurated. The Apostle Paul said that Christ Jesus "became for us wisdom from God." (1 Corinthians 1:30) For the first three centuries, the church viewed the waging of war as incompatible with following Christ, not because they were ethical pacifists, but simply because they belonged to the kingdom that shall learn war no more. For the early Christians, war belonged to the antiquated kingdoms of the world that had not yet submitted to the reign of Christ—war was now an abolished and antichrist anachronism. Christians, by virtue of their baptism, belong to the age to come. Whether or not the kingdoms of the fallen world acknowledge the Lordship of Christ is irrelevant to us. We who confess that Jesus is Lord are obligated to live according to the dictates of Christ's kingdom here and now. For the baptized, Isaiah's "days to come" arrived with Christ.

God of the holy prophets, help us to see that we have inherited what the prophets could only foretell. Strengthen us to live as a peaceable people in a world still at war. O Lord, may we walk in the light of Christ here and now. Amen.

First Week of Advent

Tuesday

Isaiah 7:1–17

Immanuel

In the year 735 BC Jerusalem was under threat from a northern alliance of Damascus and Samaria. In dread of the impending attack, we're told that the heart of King Ahaz and the heart of the people of Jerusalem "shook as the trees of the forest before the wind." The king was inspecting the water supply of Jerusalem in anticipation of a long siege when the prophet Isaiah found him. Isaiah told Ahaz not to be afraid, but to stand firm in faith because the anticipated attack would not come to pass. The prophet then instructed the king to ask God for a sign and to make it big—"let it be deep as Sheol or high as heaven." When Ahaz declined, the prophet said God himself would give the sign guaranteeing Jerusalem's salvation. Isaiah identified a pregnant young woman— presumably Ahaz's wife—and said this will be the sign: The child will be a boy and by the time he's weaned Damascus and Samaria will no longer be a threat to

Jerusalem. The child was to be named Immanuel because "God is with us." Two years later Damascus and Samaria were invaded by Assyria and were no longer a threat to Jerusalem. By 733 BC Isaiah and Ahaz thought the Immanuel prophecy was fulfilled…but they were wrong. The prophet had said more than even he realized.

A young woman had a baby boy named Immanuel, just as Isaiah had said, and the threat of invasion was soon nullified. The prophecy was apparently fulfilled. The sign was impressive enough, but was it really as deep as Sheol and as high as heaven? It turns out that the prophecy was much more than what Isaiah or Ahaz or anyone could have imagined. No one knew it then, but seven centuries later the Immanuel prophecy would find its greater fulfillment—and it would be as high as heaven and as deep as Sheol.

When we get to the fourth Sunday of Advent, we'll look at the virgin birth of Christ, but here in Isaiah 7 we find the hidden anticipation of it. No one could have *predicted* that Messiah would be born of a virgin from reading Isaiah 7, but once we know that Christ, the true Immanuel, was born, not just of a young woman as it says in the Hebrew text, but of a *virgin* as it says in the Greek Septuagint, then we can see it. When the first Christians read Isaiah 7 in their Greek Bibles, they said, "There it is! The prophecy of the virgin birth!" It's only by reading the Scriptures in the light of Christ that we access their full meaning—a meaning that is deep as Sheol and as high as heaven. For Isaiah, Immanuel meant that God is on our side; but for Matthew, Immanuel meant that God had actually joined humanity. With the full telling of the gospel we hear how Immanuel came from heaven and descended to hell that he might heal humanity and span heaven and hell with the salvation of God.

O God, we thank you that in Christ you have become Immanuel—God with us. And we praise you, O God, that your salvation reaches to the heights of heaven and to the depths of hell. Amen.

First Week of Advent
Wednesday

Isaiah 9:1–7
Unto Us A Child Is Born

The land of Galilee had the cruel misfortune to be situated in a corridor connecting the great northern and southern empires of the ancient Near East, so that it was frequently subjected to "the boots of the tramping warriors." The fertile fields of Galilee were too often turned into bloody battlefields. The city of Megiddo in the heart of the Jezreel valley was destroyed by war an astounding twenty-six times. The valley of Megiddo (Armageddon) would eventually become a grim poetic way of speaking of war itself. No doubt there was plenty of gloom and anguish in the land of Zebulun and Naphtali in the days of Isaiah. But the poet imagines a future when those living in the gloom of Galilee would see a great light and rejoice as people do when a long war is finally over. And the poem tells us that this great day of light and joy will be brought about by the birth of a child.

Clearly Isaiah is anticipating the birth of Messiah—a spirit-anointed king from the line of David who will restore the kingdom of Israel to its former and future glory. This restored Davidic kingdom will be characterized by deep justice and ever-increasing shalom. Isaiah is confident that it will come to pass because Yahweh himself is zealous to bring it to pass. The prophet heaps four laudatory titles upon the messianic child: Wonderful Counselor, Mighty God, Everlasting Father, Prince of Peace. And though he doesn't expressly say so, we can probably assume that Isaiah had pinned his hopes on Hezekiah, the son of King Ahaz, as the messianic child "born unto us." Hezekiah did turn out to be a rare good king of Judah, but he wasn't the Messiah. It would be a long wait for the arrival of the true Prince of Peace.

It's only in the light of Christ that we can look back upon Isaiah's poem and fully appreciate its prophetic significance. For example, when Isaiah says, "the government shall be upon his shoulders," we would at first regard this as a poetic way of saying that the messianic king will possess full authority. But in the light of Christ we see the cross—for indeed the cross *is* the government of God! Christ does not rule apart from the cross, but from the cross. The shape of Christ's government is eternally cruciform. Messiah is not just another king ruling with a sword—that would keep the world in the gloom and anguish of Iron Age Galilee. It's when Jesus began to preach the good news of the peaceable kingdom that the messianic light began to shine in Galilee.

Matthew tells us that Isaiah's prophecy of a light shining in Galilee is fulfilled when Jesus withdrew to Galilee and made his home in Capernaum by the sea, in the territory of Zebulun and Naphtali, because "from that time Jesus began to preach, saying, 'Repent for the kingdom of heaven has come near.'" (Matthew 4:17)

Lord Jesus, we confess that you truly are the Prince of Peace and that the government upon your shoulders is the cross you bore. Give us grace to walk in the light of the cross that we might live as subjects of the King who is Wonderful Counselor, Mighty God, Everlasting Father, and Prince of Peace. Amen.

First Week of Advent
Thursday

Isaiah 11:1–5, 10
The Root of Jesse

A few years ago, a Palestinian Christian in Bethlehem gave me an Orthodox icon as a gift. This beautiful icon that now sits in my study depicts Jesus as an olive tree with prominent people from his genealogy sprouting from the branches. Some versions of the icon depict the tree growing up out of a sleeping man—Jesse, the father of King David and the progenitor of the Davidic line. The icon, known as the "Tree of Jesse," is derived from our Advent scripture reading for today.

Isaiah begins his Root of Jesse poem with the image of a dead stump representing the royal line of the Davidic monarchy. A tree that once promised to fill Israel with the fruit of righteousness and justice is now just a dead stump. The dead stump speaks of the deep failure of the Davidic dynasty. The line began promisingly with King David, a man after God's own heart, reached an apex of glory with King Solomon, but then began to degenerate in the third generation with the egotistical and inept reign of King Rehoboam. Now in its third century the line of David is a dead stump—instead of producing the fruit of God's justice, it's just another corrupt monarchy.

But in the face of spent hope and dashed dreams, the prophet imagines a marvelous thing. Out of the dry stump a green and flourishing shoot begins to grow. The stump of Jesse's tree is not as dead as it seems—from the royal line hope will spring anew in the form of a new and anointed son of David. Isaiah prophecies that the Spirit will rest upon this future king in a sevenfold way so that that the king himself is like a seven-branched menorah. This new shoot from Jesse will be anointed with the spirit of Yahweh, the spirit of wisdom, the spirit of understanding, the spirit of counsel, the spirit of might, the spirit of knowledge, and the spirit of the fear of the Lord.

The result of the sevenfold anointing on the Root of Jesse will be a revival of justice. In Isaiah's day the poor had been denied their rights and were subject to the predatory practices of wealthy landowners—a sin that Isaiah unflinchingly depicts and scathingly denounces in his early poems. "Woe to you who buy up house after house and field after field, until everyone is evicted and you live all alone in the land." (Isaiah 5:8) But now Isaiah finds hope as he envisions a revival of the righteous line of David with a new king who will rule with the force of his word and bring about justice and fair treatment for the poor and exploited.

Eight centuries after Isaiah, in his letter to the believers in Rome, the Apostle Paul identified Jesus Christ as the promised Root of Jesse and the hope of the Gentiles: "And again Isaiah says, 'The Root of Jesse shall come, even he who arises to rule the Gentiles; in him the Gentiles shall hope.'" (Romans 15:12)

Lord Jesus Christ, you are the Root of Jesse, the true Son of David, the one in whom we hope. O Lord, bring the righteous rule of your word into our world and in your faithfulness execute justice for the poor and exploited. Amen.

FIRST WEEK OF ADVENT
FRIDAY

Isaiah 11:6–9
The Lion and the Lamb

Isaiah's messianic poems are filled with what we have come to think of as Christmas themes—the virgin conceiving, a child named Immanuel, the reign of the Prince of Peace. In today's reading we find the lion lying down with the lamb. In this remarkable passage the poet employs zoomorphism as he imagines the human world as an animal kingdom. When my children were young one of their favorite movies was Disney's animated *Robin Hood*. They watched it countless times. In this cartoon the human characters are depicted as animals: the clever Robin Hood is a fox; the villainous Prince John is a lion and his devious assistant is a snake; the lovable Friar Tuck is a badger and the dangerous sheriff of Nottingham is a wolf; the good guys are animals like rabbits and turtles, while the bad guys are vultures and crocodiles. The zoomorphism of Disney's *Robin Hood* is more or less what Isaiah is doing with his powerful prophetic imagination.

If we literalize the poem and try to imagine carnivores turning into herbivores, we miss the whole point. Isaiah isn't worried about lions eating antelopes (that's not what's wrong with the world); Isaiah is worried about the predation enacted by human predators. As we have already seen, Isaiah is deeply concerned about the rich and powerful preying upon the poor and vulnerable. In God's creation it is acceptable for beasts to behave beastly (for the lion to devour the lamb), but it is not acceptable for humans bearing the image of God to behave beastly.

Isaiah depicts the beastly exploitation of the poor and vulnerable by the rich and powerful as something transformed by the righteous reign of the Root of Jesse. By his word Messiah will bring about a change in the hearts and minds of human beasts. Instead of behaving beastly toward the vulnerable, they will behave humanely. Or to put it more poetically, the lion will lie down with the lamb!

But do lions really ever lie down with lambs? Yes, they do! We see it in the ministry of Jesus. Zacchaeus, the chief tax collector in Jericho, was a wolf who worked for the Roman beast and got rich by cheating the poor. But when Jesus came to his house, the wolf in his heart was slain. When Zacchaeus pledged to give away half of his fortune and make four-fold restitution, the wolf was lying down with the lamb. Saul of Tarsus was a lion violently devouring the flock of God, but when he encountered Jesus on the Damascus road, he not only stopped attacking the flock, he became a faithful shepherd. In Christ Isaiah's dream comes true and the lion really does lie down with the Lamb. If the world is still dangerous because human predators behaving beastly toward the vulnerable, it is because the earth is not yet full of the knowledge of the Lord as the waters cover the sea...so we continue to pray.

Lord Jesus, we long for the day when your knowledge covers the earth as the waters cover the sea, so that at long last the lion will lie down with the lamb. As John the Revelator foresaw, may the peaceable kingdom of the Lamb prevail over the beastly kingdoms of this age. Amen.

First Week of Advent
Saturday

Isaiah 25:6–9
The Great Feast of God

After a long series of polemic poems pronouncing Yahweh's judgment on Judah's enemies—Babylon, Assyria, Philistia, Moab, Damascus, Ethiopia, Egypt, Tyre, and finally the entire Gentile world—Isaiah now composes a poem against the greatest enemy of all: Death itself. Isaiah imagines Yahweh preparing a great feast on Mount Zion in celebration of death's destruction. The poet tells us that a burial shroud has been cast over all peoples and that a sheet has been pulled over the corpse of all nations. This is the tyranny of death that threatens to make life meaningless. But now Yahweh has acted and the burial shroud has been turned into a tablecloth for the great feast of God. The funeral bier has been transformed into a banqueting table laden with the finest food and wine. The funeral has become a feast! Isaiah's stunning eschatological hope proclaims that when death has been swallowed up forever, God will wipe away the tears from all faces. John the Revelator incorporates Isaiah's poem in the culmination of his grand vision:

> And God will wipe away every tear from
>   their eyes.
> Death shall be no more;
> neither shall there be mourning, nor
>   crying, nor pain anymore,
> for the former things have passed away.
> (Revelation 21:4)

In this poem Isaiah anticipates a day when death will be destroyed by God and the heirs of salvation will rejoice and say, "This is what we've been waiting for!" And that's what Advent is all about—anticipating and waiting. But as those who believe that the anticipated Christ has arrived in the person of Jesus of Nazareth, we are invited to live in the joyful tension of the "now and not yet." While we await the final redemption of all things in Christ, we celebrate the fact that the feast has already begun. The feast of rich food and fine wine on Mount Zion began on the night when Jesus gathered in the Upper Room with his disciples and said, "This is my body" and "This is my blood." Indeed, the Eucharistic feast is the feast that celebrates the destruction of death and the gift of eternal life. Listen to how Jesus talks to us about his flesh and blood:

> Very truly, I tell you, unless you eat the flesh of the Son of Man and drink his blood, you have no life in you. Those who eat my flesh and drink my blood have eternal life, and I will raise them up on the last day; my flesh is true food and my blood is true drink. Those who eat my flesh and drink my blood abide in me, and I in them. Just as the living Father sent me, and I live because of the Father, so whoever eats me will live because of me. (John 6:53–57)

Tomorrow when we come to the Communion table, we will have arrived at the great feast of God foretold by Isaiah!

Lord Jesus, your flesh and blood are indeed the great feast of God. We thank you that in the Communion meal we find the feast of eternal life. Amen.

SECOND WEEK OF ADVENT

SUNDAY

Isaiah 35:1–10

Here Is Your God

When Isaiah penned his "Rivers In the Desert" poem, Judah was in a bad way—internally Judah was corrupt and externally it was under threat of foreign invasion. But the poet of audacious hope does not despair; instead he proclaims that God will come, and in that day it will be said, "Here is your God!" And what happens when God comes? Isaiah first paints a picture of a dry and barren desert flourishing, then switches the image from the environment being healed to people being healed. On the day that God comes the blind will see, the deaf will hear, the dumb will speak, and the lame will leap. At the end of the poem Isaiah returns to his zoomorphic literary device and speaks of a highway that runs through the now flourishing desert where there will be no beastly tyrants to disturb the peace and safety of the righteous who are traveling to Zion singing their songs of salvation. The healing wrought by the arrival of God is so complete that even sorrow and sighing flee away. Someday it will be said, "Here is your God" and on that day all that is wrong will be set right. But for now, all we can do is wait.

And that's what Advent is for—learning to wait for God. In our high-tech, high-speed, high-stress age, we're not very good at waiting—it feels too much like doing nothing. But it's not doing nothing. As we wait, we slowly become contemplative enough to discern what God is doing. Unless we intentionally cultivate some contemplative slowness in our soul, it doesn't matter if God acts, because we will most likely miss it. When God entered history definitively in Christ, a lot of people who should have perceived it and rejoiced, missed what God was doing or even resisted it. Quiet contemplatives like Simeon and Anna perceived the arrival of God's salvation because they had learned how to wait.

The deeper truth is that God is always acting, because God is always loving his creation. The Father, Son, and Holy Spirit are always inviting us into their house of love. But when we are consumed by anger, harried by anxiety, and driven by impatience, we are blind and deaf to what God is actually doing in the present moment. God is always about to act in our life and in our world, but if we want to discern the actions of God we must learn to first wait in quiet contemplation. Advent is a season to keep watch and ponder the stars like the ancient magi, to keep vigil in the fields like the shepherds of Bethlehem. God is always about to act and God is always acting. The question is, can we perceive it? Another poem in Isaiah sums it up well:

> Behold, I am about to do a new thing;
> now it springs forth.
> Do you not perceive it?
> I will make a way in the wilderness
> and rivers in the desert.
> (Isaiah 43:19)

O God, you are always about to act and bring about a new thing; help us to wait patiently, that we might perceive and welcome what you bring to pass. Amen.

SECOND WEEK OF ADVENT
MONDAY

Isaiah 40:1–2
Comfort Ye My People

The book of Isaiah is like a mini-Bible. Just as the Bible is divided into a first Testament with thirty-nine books and a second Testament with twenty-seven books, so Isaiah consists of two halves: the first thirty-nine chapters written in Jerusalem before the exile and the final twenty-seven chapters written in Babylon during the exile. Between the two halves is a kind of "intertestamental period" of about a century and a half. In the gap between the poems of Isaiah of Jerusalem (1–39) and Isaiah of the Exile (40–66) is where the book of Lamentations is situated chronologically. Lamentations is a collection of poems attributed to Jeremiah that give artistic expression to the grief that came upon the Jewish people in 587 BC when Jerusalem was destroyed and the population deported to Babylon. One of the recurring themes in Lamentations is that there is no one to offer comfort:

She weeps bitterly in the night
With tears on her cheeks,
She has **none to comfort**.

Her downfall was terrible,
With **none to comfort**.

Zion stretches out her hands,
But there is **none to comfort**.

They heard my groaning,
But there was **none to comfort**.
(Lamentations 1:2, 9, 17, 21)

But at last comfort has come. The first line of
Isaiah of the Exile's first poem begins with "Comfort ye,
comfort ye my people." And with good reason these are
the first words in Handel's Messiah. The second half of
Isaiah is so full of gospel themes that it is often described
as the Fifth Gospel. Because this is an Advent devotional,
I have selected mostly hopeful readings from First Isaiah,
but the reality is that there are a lot of "woes." Of the
twenty-two "woes" in the book of Isaiah, all but two are

in the first part. But with First Isaiah behind us, the woes have been pronounced, judgment has been threatened, catastrophe has fallen, and now it is time to comfort the people of God.

In 1902, American journalist Finley Peter Dunne said, "The job of the newspaper man is to comfort the afflicted and afflict the comfortable." I don't know if that's really the job of the journalist, but it's certainly the job of the prophet. Isaiah of Jerusalem had to afflict the comfortable elite of Jerusalem by confronting their idolatry and injustice with his scathing woes. But Isaiah of the Exile has a different task. Impoverished and grief-stricken exiles living as a vulnerable minority in the midst of a foreign superpower don't need woes, they need comfort. And so in his first poem, Isaiah speaks tenderly to the exiles saying, "Your warfare is ended, your sins are pardoned, and the time of comfort has drawn near."

As we enter Second Isaiah and the second week of Advent, now might be a good time to listen to the Christmas portion of Handel's Messiah and receive it for what it is—God's word of comfort for an afflicted people.

O God, in our affliction we look to you for comfort; send us the word from heaven that will revive our hope and restore our soul. Amen.

Second Week of Advent

Tuesday

Isaiah 40:3–11

Prepare the Way

Isaiah of the Exile has been commissioned by God to bring comfort to the people of Israel, and his message of comfort is that God is coming. Isaiah reports that Yahweh, who seemed to have abandoned Judea and gone into exile, is about to return to Jerusalem. From the highest mountain this good news is to be proclaimed: "Do not fear! God is coming!" But with what disposition is God coming? God is coming as a gentle shepherd who will gather his flock, feed his flock, and lead his flock. "He will gather the lambs in his arms and carry them in his bosom." Isaiah has become a herald of good tidings and his task is to *go tell it on the mountain!*

In response to the good news, Israel is to prepare the way. If God is coming, the way should be made easy for his arrival—valleys are to be lifted up, mountains made low, hills made level, and rough places made smooth. An interstate highway for the coming glory of

God is to be constructed. These are the road metaphors the poet uses as he urges his hearers to prepare their hearts for the arrival of their salvation. And how will this salvation come? It will come as the word of God. Frail humanity has failed them—kings and princes, priests and people have all failed and Israel has been led into exile. Human constancy is like grass—the grass that withers and the flower that fades. But now God is about to end the exile and send his word—his enduring word that is unencumbered by human frailty. From this very first of Isaiah of the Exile's poems we gain powerful messianic expectations. Thus it should be no surprise that Mark, the first Gospel written, begins with Isaiah 40.

The beginning of the gospel of Jesus Christ, the Son of God, as it is written in the prophet Isaiah:

> Behold, I am sending my messenger before you,
> who will prepare your way;
> the voice of one crying in the wilderness:
> "Prepare the way of the Lord."
> (Mark 1:1–3)

And so John the Baptist appeared in the Judean wilderness, preaching a message of repentance in preparation for the coming of Messiah. John also baptized people in the Jordan river, not only as a public act of repentance, but also as a symbolic re-entry into the promised land. John's baptism said this: We are returning from our exile in sin; we are rethinking our ways of idolatry and injustice; we are preparing our hearts for the arrival our true king.

This is exactly what we are doing during Advent—we are preparing our hearts for a new arrival of Christ in our lives. We are lifting up the valleys of our low view of others; we are bringing down the mountains of pride; we are smoothing out our rough and uncharitable attitudes, all in preparation to receive the Word of God into our lives in a new way.

O God, our constancy is like the grass that withers and the flower the fades. Have mercy and send us your unchanging Word who is Jesus Christ. By your Holy Spirit help us to prepare the way for the coming of our salvation. Amen.

SECOND WEEK OF ADVENT
WEDNESDAY

Isaiah 42:1–9
A Light to the Nations

Beginning today and for the next six days we will look at the Servant Songs in Isaiah. The Servant Songs are four poems that depict Israel as Yahweh's servant to whom promises are given and concerning whom predictions are made. And though it is clear that the servant is Israel, the personification of Israel as Yahweh's servant is always presented as an individual. As such, there is nothing in the Old Testament that more clearly informs messianic expectations than the Servant Songs of Isaiah. When we look at these four poems as a whole we can ask and answer an enormously important question: Who is the Messiah? Messiah is Israel embodied in one person who fulfills Israel's vocation and is glorified among the nations, but who also suffers greatly in the accomplishment of this task.

In the first Servant Song we are told that Yahweh takes delight in the Servant and places his spirit upon him.

The task of this beloved and anointed Servant is to bring about justice—to set right a world gone wrong. And the establishment of Yahweh's justice through the work of the Servant will not be limited to Israel but will reach to the Gentile nations. The Gentiles, characterized by their idolatry, are depicted as prisoners held captive in a dark dungeon. The Servant comes to the aid of these prisoners by illuminating their darkness and releasing them from their captivity. What is being said is that Israel, as embodied by the Servant, will someday liberate the Gentile world from their spiritual blindness and bondage to idolatry. The most remarkable thing Isaiah says in this song is that the Servant will be "given as a covenant to the people." Isaiah does not explain what this means, but it seems full of portent.

As great as he obviously is, there is nothing haughty or pretentious about the Servant—the greatness of the Servant will not be in the ostentatious manner of the Gentile kings and conquerors. Though the teaching of the Servant will reach the ends of the earth, he will go about his task with humility and quiet gentleness. With the consummate skill of a refined poet, Isaiah says, "a bruised reed he will not break, and a smoldering wick he will not quench." So it is no wonder that Matthew draws upon Isaiah's first Servant Song to comment on the quiet humility of Jesus as he went about his ministry.

> When Jesus became aware of this, he departed. Many crowds followed him, and he cured them, and he ordered them not to make him known. This was to fulfill what had been spoken through the prophet Isaiah: "Here is my servant, whom I have chosen...he will not break a bruised reed or quench a smoldering wick until he brings justice to victory. And in his name the Gentiles will hope." (Matthew 12:15–21)

Lord Jesus, you are the gentle and humble Servant of God who has become the light of the nations. O Lord, our fidelity is often like a bruised reed and our faith like a smoldering wick; please deal gently with us as you bring your justice to victory. Amen.

SECOND WEEK OF ADVENT

THURSDAY

Isaiah 49:1–7

Salvation to the Ends of the Earth

The second of Isaiah's Servant Songs begins in the voice of the Servant himself. The Servant—Yahweh's Chosen One who personally takes up and fulfills Israel's vocation—addresses himself to the Gentile world, poetically described as "coastlands" and "peoples from afar." The servant announces, "Yahweh has made my mouth like a sharp sword." John the Revelator draws upon this text when he portrays Christ as the Word of God riding upon a white horse and prevailing over the nations with a sharp sword proceeding from his mouth. (See Revelation 19:11–16.)

It's clear that the Servant is destined by God to rule and save the nations, but at one point in the song the Servant expresses dismay when he says, "I have labored in vain." The servant then quickly recovers by confessing, "my cause is with the LORD." If we see the Servant

Songs as portending the mission of Messiah, we might connect this song with the Cry of Dereliction and the final entrustment of his spirit into the hands of the Father. (See Matthew 27:46 and Luke 23:46.)

In the song the Servant says that he has been formed in the womb by Yahweh, and that Yahweh has foretold the scope of the Servant's mission. Though the Servant will restore Israel's fidelity to their God, this task is too small for the greatness of the Servant. So the Servant will be sent to the Gentile nations that the salvation of Yahweh might transcend the borders of Israel and reach to the ends of the earth. Initially the Servant will be despised and abhorred by the nations, but ultimately the kings of the Gentiles shall bow before the Servant.

In 1857 John Henry Hopkins Jr., an Episcopal bishop, wrote the now famous Christmas carol, *We Three Kings*.

> We three kings of Orient are,
> Bearing gifts we traverse afar.

Matthew tells us of the Magi who came with gifts and bowed before the Christ child in Bethlehem. That their number is three is surmised from the number of their gifts, but the tradition that the Magi were also kings is derived from God's promise to his Chosen One at the end of the second Servant Song.

> Kings shall see and arise,
> Princes too shall prostrate themselves,
> Because of the LORD who is faithful,
> the Holy One of Israel, who has chosen you.

The promise of the second song is that though the Servant's mission will begin with gathering Israel back to God, it will culminate with the whole world gathered into God's salvation. Jesus told the Samaritan women at the well, "Salvation is from the Jews." (John 4:22) But after Jesus stayed in Sychar for two days, the Samaritans said, "we know that this is truly the Savior of the world." (John 4:42) Indeed, we now know that Jesus is the Jewish Messiah who has brought God's salvation to the whole world—a glorious truth that was first hinted at in Isaiah's Servant Songs.

Lord Jesus, you are the Chosen One of God who brings salvation to the ends of the earth; may the sharp sword of your word strike down all that would keep us enslaved to sin. Amen.

Second Week of Advent

Friday

Isaiah 50:4–9

A Word for the Weary

In the third Servant Song we begin to clearly see the suffering and humiliation that will befall the Servant in the course of his mission. In verse 6 the Servant says,

> I gave my back to those who beat me,
> and my cheeks to those who pulled out my beard;
> I did not hide my face from insult and spitting.

The degree to which the Servant Songs informed Jesus of his impending suffering is probably enormous. In Luke, Jesus foretells his disciples the fate of the Son of Man: "He will be handed over to the Gentiles; and he will be mocked and insulted and spat upon. And after flogging him, they will kill him." (Luke 18:32–33) Jesus knew the Servant songs and he knew the suffering that awaited him. But we will save the anticipated suffering of the Servant for the fourth song. In this meditation I want to focus on how the Servant says he knows how to "sustain the weary with a word."

When we hear the Servant speak of sustaining the weary, we are immediately reminded of one of the most beloved invitations of Jesus.

> Come to me, all you that are weary and are carrying heavy burdens, and I will give you rest. Take my yoke upon you, and learn from me; for I am gentle and humble of heart, and you will find rest for your souls. For my yoke is easy, and my burden is light. (Matthew 11:28–30)

To the weary and worn, overwhelmed with the struggles of life, Jesus says, "Come to me. You're weary and I want to give you rest. You're worn out from heavy burdens; let me lighten your load. The world is harsh, but I am gentle; the age is arrogant, but I am humble; the times are hard, but my yoke is easy. Come to me and I will give you rest."

Jesus doesn't say that when we come to him all of our burdens will magically disappear, rather Jesus invites us to *learn* from him. Jesus is the Servant who has been given the "tongue of a teacher" and wants to guide us into a new way of living—the way of radical trust. When life is too hard, we trust. When it's too heavy, we trust. When it's all too complicated, we can trust. Those who trust discover the grace of God. Eugene Peterson describes this as learning from Jesus "the unforced rhythms of grace."

Advent is a good time to begin to learn the unforced rhythms of grace, and Jesus is our teacher. I encourage you to set aside some time this weekend and sit with Jesus—simply sit down in a quiet place and welcome the presence of the Lord. Then talk to Jesus, tell him of your exhaustion and heavy burdens. And finally, listen to Jesus, for he has something to say—he has a word for the weary.

Lord Jesus, we are the weary and worn, and so at your invitation we come to you. Help us with our heavy load and our hard yoke. Merciful Lord, give us a word in season that will sustain us in our weariness. Amen.

Second Week of Advent
Saturday

Isaiah 52:13–15
Many Were Astonished at Him

For the next three days we will look at the fourth and most famous of the Servant Songs; it's with the fourth song that we most clearly see the Servant as one who suffers. Though this song may be more associated with Lent or even Good Friday than with Advent, we should understand that to properly anticipate the Christ, Isaiah's song of the Suffering Servant must be heard.

Isaiah begins his song by announcing that the Servant will succeed, prosper, and be exalted—a theme that is present in all the Servant Songs. But considering what will follow in the rest of the Song, when Isaiah says that the Servant will be "lifted up," we might see here an ominous allusion. In the final week of his ministry, Jesus spoke of his impending crucifixion as being "lifted up."

"And I, when I am lifted up from the earth, will draw all people to myself." He said this to indicate the kind of death he was to die. (John 12:32–33)

In Isaiah's song, the effect of the Servant being lifted up is that many are astonished because his appearance is so marred that he no longer resembles a human being. The sight of the Servant lifted up in a state of disfigurement startles the nations and renders kings speechless—it is a simultaneously glorious and horrible spectacle that leaves them dumbfounded. These are indeed portentous words. For Christian readers of Isaiah, they seem to be an eerie foreshadowing of Golgotha.

Beside the door to my study there is a print of *The Two Crowns*—a painting from 1900 by Sir Frank Dicksee. I've contemplated this arresting work of art many times. The painting portrays a medieval king returning in triumph from a victorious battle. The king is still in his armor, wearing a crown of gold and sitting astride a white stallion, while banners fly and women throw flowers. With his left hand the king holds the reigns of his warhorse, as his right hand rests on the hilt of his sword. But none of this is what captures the attention of the viewer. Instead, we are drawn to the surprised look on the king's face. As we follow the gaze of the king, we see that he is looking directly at a life-size crucifix. The king with a crown of gold is clearly astonished by the king with a crown of thorns—thus the title of the painting: *The Two Crowns*. The king with a crown of gold has won his kingdom by the power of the sword. But the king with the crown of thorns has won his kingdom by his death upon a cross. Dicksee's painting seems to be an artistic portrayal of Isaiah 52:15:

> He shall startle many nations,
> Kings shall shut their mouths because of
>   him.
> For that which has not been told them
>   they shall see,
> And that which they have not heard they
>   shall contemplate.

Lord Jesus, as we behold you, the King of kings, nailed to a tree, may we ever be astonished. And in our astonishment may be begin to contemplate a way of life, not dependent upon the sword, but indebted to the cross. Amen.

Third Week of Advent
Sunday

Isaiah 53:1–9
A Lamb Led to the Slaughter

This middle portion of the fourth Servant Song is the prime example of why the book of Isaiah is often called the "Fifth Gospel." The first Christians saw the suffering and vindication of Jesus throughout Isaiah 53, and thus these verses appear repeatedly in the Gospels and Epistles. Isaiah's Suffering Servant poem contain the narrative contours of the Passion story.

The Servant is depicted as the arm of Yahweh sent to bring salvation to Israel. The Servant does not arrive in a moment of majestic grandeur, but grows up in quiet obscurity—so obscure that one might ask if anything notable could come out of, say, a tiny village like Nazareth? As the Servant becomes a public figure, he is ultimately rejected and despised, wounded and bruised, oppressed and afflicted. Finally the Servant is put to death. It is presumed that his burial will be with the criminals, but strangely his tomb is with the rich. When we hear these words, how can we not think of the hill of Golgotha and the garden of Joseph of Arimathea?

One of the things that stands out in the song is how the Servant is made a scapegoat. Through the satanic phenomenon of blame, the mob projects their own sins upon the Servant who has now become their scapegoat. Isaiah describes it like this: "He was wounded because of our transgressions and bruised because of our iniquities." The mob attacking the scapegoat assumes that the Servant is being stricken and punished by God, but the prophet knows better, describing the awful events as a "perversion of justice."

Through the greatest injustice the innocent Servant is made a vilified scapegoat, but he does not open his mouth in protest. Instead, he comports himself as a lamb led to the slaughter—for indeed, this is the Lamb of God who takes away the sin of the world! The sin of the nation—yea, the sin of the world—was unjustly laid upon the sinless Lamb, and the Lamb bears it in silence that it might be forgiven en masse.

The First Epistle of Peter draws directly from Isaiah 53 to describe the salvific work of Christ's suffering.

He committed no sin, and no deceit was found in his mouth. When he was abused, he did not return abuse; when he suffered, he did not threaten, but he entrusted himself to the one who judges justly. He himself bore our sins in his body on the cross, so that we, free from sins, might live for righteousness. By his wounds you have been healed. (1 Peter 2:22–24)

The Apostle looks to the song of the Suffering Servant to express how the cross of Christ saves us, and he sums it up with these poignant words: "By his wounds you have been healed." On Good Friday the sin of the world fatally wounded the Servant of God. But the Servant did not threaten or retaliate; instead, he absorbed the blow and forgave it all. I know no better atonement theory than this: By his wounds we are healed.

Lord Jesus, you are the Lamb of God who takes away the sin of the world. And so we bring our woundedness to your holy wounds that we might be healed. Amen.

THIRD WEEK OF ADVENT
MONDAY

Isaiah 53:10–12
He Bore the Sin of Many

Today we come to the conclusion of the fourth and final Servant Song—the song of the Suffering Servant. In the middle portion of the song, the poet asks how the unjustly executed Servant could have a future, but in the closing lines of the song we are told that the Servant does indeed have a future—a glorious future. Even though earlier in the poem Isaiah has spoken of the death of the Servant ("They made his grave with the wicked and his tomb with the rich"), the poet now says that Yahweh will "prolong his days." The conclusion of the poem speaks both of the death of the Servant ("he poured out himself unto death") and his glorious future ("he shall see his offspring"). Though I would not describe this as a sixth-century BC prediction of resurrection that could prognosticate Easter, in the light of Easter the words "prolong his days" takes on a new and wonderful meaning.

The glorious theme at the end of the fourth Servant Song is the implication that the suffering of the Servant is inextricably connected with the forgiveness of Israel and the world. The poem ends with these words: "He bore the sin of many, and made intercession for the transgressors." Again, I'm not sure how one in the time of Isaiah would understand or interpret these words, but for the Christian there seems to be a direct line to Luke 23:34—"Father, forgive them, for they know not what they do." This petition from the cross is the Servant making intercession for the transgressors. Christ's prayer, "Father, forgive them," is not the Son acting as an agent of change upon the Father; rather it is the Son revealing the eternal, immutable heart of the Father as one of boundless forgiveness. As Jesus said, "Whatever the Father does, the Son does likewise," and "The Father and I are one." (John 5:19, 10:30) The cross is not what God inflicts upon Christ in order to forgive; the cross is what God in Christ endures as he forgives. The cross is not where God punishes his Son; the cross is where God in Christ endures and forgives an unjust punishment inflicted by a sinful world.

Yet some have stumbled over this as they read in verse 10, "Yet it pleased the LORD to crush him." We gain a better understanding that is in keeping with the whole song when we read this verse in the Septuagint— the Greek Translation of the Hebrew Scriptures that was predominate in the time of Christ, and used by the New Testament writers. The Septuagint translates Isaiah 53:10 like this: "The Lord is willing to cleanse him of the injury." Was God pleased with the torture and crucifixion of his beloved Son? Of course not. That would be to say that God is pleased with sin. What pleased the Father was to "cleanse him of the injury"—that is, to raise him from the dead and undo by resurrection what sin had done by crucifixion. This is the gospel.

Lord Jesus, we praise you that you have borne the sin of many, and made intercession for us by your eternal prayer, "Father, forgive them." Amen.

Third Week of Advent
Tuesday

Isaiah 55:1–13
The Word from Heaven

The Jewish exiles in Babylon will soon be allowed to return to Jerusalem, but after fifty years in exile, many of them are about to "return" to a place they've never been, and Isaiah wants them to understand that "home" is a very different place than Babylon. So Isaiah evokes the image of a street vendor hawking his wares. The street vendor has wine and milk—symbols of abundance. *Milk and wine for sale!* But in Babylon the Jewish exiles cannot afford these tokens of abundance. They're exiles, immigrants, cheap labor, the underclass— the "good life" in Babylon is out of their reach. So now Yahweh is depicted as a street vendor crying out, *Are you thirsty? I have milk and wine! Take your pick! You don't need money! It's all free!* It's clear that the exiles' new home is to be very different from Babylon. For one thing it runs on an entirely different economy—an economy of generosity, not exploitation.

Babylon (as the biblical archetype of empire) insists that its way is not only the best way, it's the only way. Prophetic imagination of an alternative society based in generosity is censored. Everything in Babylon serves the exclusive paradigm of consumerism and militarism. But now Isaiah informs the exiles headed for home that the ways of Yahweh operate on a level they have not yet comprehended.

> For as the heavens are higher than the earth,
> So are my ways higher than your ways
> And my thoughts than your thoughts.

Because all the exiles have ever known is the consumerist militarism of Babylon, they cannot fathom an alternative based in shalom. But God is going to send his word from heaven—a word they can't imagine—and this word will not return empty, it will succeed. Isaiah's poem ends by saying that as the exiles return in peace, the mountains will break into song and the trees will applaud their return. Painful things like thorns and briers will be replaced with pleasant things like the cypress and myrtle. This is the end of exile.

But when the Jewish exiles began to return home in 539 BC, were they really home? They were still dominated by foreign powers—the Persian Empire, the Seleucid Empire, the Roman Empire. Maybe the word from heaven that succeeds in its purpose is not a sermon or song from Isaiah, but something else. Maybe the word from heaven that ends the exile is the Word made flesh.

> No one has ascended into heaven except
> the one who descended from heaven, the
> Son of Man. ... For God did not send his
> Son into the world to condemn the world,
> but to save the world through him. (John
> 3:13, 17)

Jesus is the Word of God sent from heaven to save the world. And thus the world will be saved, because this Word will not return to God without accomplishing the purpose for which it was sent! During Advent let us remember that we are not waiting for the world to be destroyed, but for the world to be saved by Jesus Christ.

Holy Father, we thank you that the world will be saved because you have sent your Word, your Son, to save the world. Amen.

THIRD WEEK OF ADVENT
WEDNESDAY

Isaiah 61:1–11
The Good News of Messiah

In this poem Isaiah speaks in the voice of the Anointed One—the Messiah. The spirit of Yahweh is upon Messiah to bring good news (gospel) to the oppressed, the brokenhearted, the captives, the prisoners. These are the Jewish exiles who are brokenhearted over the loss of Jerusalem and their temple and have become oppressed captive prisoners in Babylon. By the spirit of Yahweh, Messiah announces the good news of healing, liberation, and restoration. This all comes about in the year of Yahweh's favor and in the day of his vengeance upon Israel's enemies. We might describe this as the political platform of Messiah—liberation and restoration, divine favor and divine vengeance. Isaiah envisions Messiah's gospel as culminating in a Jubilee of blessing upon Israel and a doomsday of retribution upon their Gentile enemies.

And then five hundred years go by…

When Jesus was baptized in the River Jordan by John the Baptist, the Holy Spirit in the form of a dove descended upon him. After forty days in the wilderness, Jesus returned to Galilee in the power of the Spirit and began to proclaim the gospel of the kingdom. The poor heard good news, the sick were healed, and the captives were set free. Eventually Jesus returned to his hometown of Nazareth. On the Sabbath he went into the synagogue where he was given the scroll of Isaiah. Jesus found the place where it is written,

> The Spirit of the Lord is upon me,
> because he has anointed me
> to bring good news to the poor.
> He has sent me to proclaim release to the captives
> and recovery of sight to the blind,
> to let the oppressed go free,
> to proclaim the year of the Lord's favor.
> (Luke 4:18–19)

Then Jesus rolled up the scroll, sat down, and announced: "Today this scripture has been fulfilled in your hearing." Following this reading, Jesus preached a sermon about God's favor bestowed upon *all* by drawing upon two stories from the Bible where God showed favor to Gentiles—the widow of Zarephath and the Syrian general Naaman. Jesus had intentionally omitted the line about God's vengeance in Isaiah's prophecy and had instead insisted that the arrival of the kingdom of God brings a Jubilee of divine favor available to all! According to Jesus, Isaiah's prophecy about the anointed Messiah was *fulfilled* with his proclamation of *good* news. Jesus' gospel had no room for revenge.

How did the people of Nazareth receive Jesus' edit and recasting of Isaiah's vision by closing the book on vengeance? Not well. In fact, they tried to throw him off a cliff. It's amazing how angry some people can become if you try to take away their religion of revenge. But Jesus calls us to something better—Jesus calls us to a gospel of grace that is good news for all people! Jubilee does not have to be accompanied by doomsday.

Lord Jesus, help us to close the book on vengeance in our own theology. Help us learn from you how to renounce revenge and embrace the good news of God's salvation for everyone. Amen.

Third Week of Advent

Thursday

Micah 5:2–4

O Little Town of Bethlehem

The prophet Micah was a contemporary of Isaiah of Jerusalem, prophesying seven hundred years before Christ. Micah is best known to us as the one who foretold the birth of Messiah in Bethlehem. Of course, Bethlehem was the birthplace of King David, so it makes sense that the messianic Son of David would also be born there. Nevertheless, Bethlehem was only a small and seemingly insignificant village, but this is in keeping with the ways of God—the work of God often emerges from quiet obscurity.

Before the village was known as Bethlehem (House of Bread), it was identified as Ephrathah (Ash Heap). It was here that Rachel, Jacob's beloved wife, died in childbirth and was buried. To this day the tomb of Rachel is located right outside the entrance to Bethlehem. Do we see a hint of the gospel in this? The ash heap of

sorrow and loss can become the place where the Bread of
Life is born.

Micah prophesies that the one whose origin is
from the Ancient of Days destined to rule Israel will be
born in Bethlehem—a village known as "the little one of
the clans of Judah." Like his father David, the Messiah
born in Bethlehem will also be a shepherd, feeding his
flock in the strength of Yahweh. And though he hails from
the smallest village in Judah, Micah says he will become
"great to the ends of the earth." The Bethlehem portion of
Micah's poem ends with the prophet saying, "And this
one shall be our peace." What an amazing prophecy this
is. Indeed, the little town of Bethlehem is famous the
world over because the Prince of Peace was born there.
Yet the prophecy is still unfolding because we are still
learning to follow our peaceful Shepherd.

I've been to Bethlehem more than twenty times.
I have Palestinian Christian friends who live there. I love
spending time in the ancient Church of the Nativity that
venerates the traditional birthplace of Christ. On my
writing desk I have a beautiful cross icon that I obtained
at one of Bethlehem's olive wood stores. I've found peace
and beauty in Bethlehem. But I've also seen separation
walls, rubber bullets, and teargas canisters there. Situated

on the fault line of one of the world's most intractable conflicts, Bethlehem lies at the intersection of iconic beauty and painful reality. The Christmas carol about Bethlehem says it just right—"the hopes and fears of all the years are met in thee tonight."

Christ is not just born in the beautiful places of our lives, as if we live in the idyllic bubble of a snow globe. Christ is also born in the war-torn places of our lives, littered with rubber bullets and teargas canisters. Jesus was not born into a fairytale but into the world as it is. And so during Advent we hold to Micah's ancient prophecy,

> He shall be great to the ends of the earth,
> And this one shall be our peace.

O King born in Bethlehem, may you come to the broken and war-torn parts of our world; be our shepherd who leads us into the ways of peace. Amen.

Third Week of Advent
Friday

Mark 1:1
The Beginning of the Gospel

Today we turn to the New Testament and for the next three weeks will look at the narratives in the Gospels pertaining to the birth of Christ. The New Testament opens with four Gospel witnesses to the life of Jesus Christ. Each Gospel has its own voice, style, perspective, and particular emphasis. The Gospels are not mere biographies in the modern sense but are theologically driven documents. The four Evangelists are not journalists but theologians. The Gospels differ in detail because Matthew, Mark, Luke, and John are more interested in theological reflection than journalistic historicity.

In the second century, the Syrian theologian Tatian, in a strangely modern move, created a single "harmonized" Gospel in an effort to smooth out any historical discrepancies. But the church, led by Irenaeus, the bishop of Lyon, wisely rejected Tatian's idea. The church understood that the collection of four distinct theological reflections on the life of Jesus is superior to a single edited and harmonized compromise.

The first Gospel to appear in the early church was Mark (even though Matthew appears first in the canonical arrangement). Tradition says Mark was the interpreter for the Apostle Peter who was the primary source for Mark's Gospel. The Gospel may have been written in Rome shortly after 70 CE. Mark tells us nothing of the birth or childhood of Jesus but launches straight into John the Baptist and the baptism of Jesus. As the first Evangelist to put quill to parchment, Mark is in a hurry! There is an excited, breathless pace to his Gospel—Mark has urgent news to tell us and there is to be no delay. Mark's recurring word is "immediately," and he uses the literary devise of dramatic present tense over one hundred fifty times. There is a palpable excitement in Mark's Gospel.

Today's reading is only one verse: "The beginning of the gospel of Jesus Christ, the Son of God." To our ears this may sound as nothing more than an innocuous introduction but it is far from that. It's actually an explosive sentence designed to startle us. To help gain an understanding of exactly how explosive it is, consider this imperial inscription placed in the city of Priene around the time of Jesus' birth.

> The birthday of the god Caesar Augustus has been for the whole world the beginning of the gospel. Therefore let all recognize a new era beginning from his birth.

In his first sentence Mark has thrown down the gauntlet—it is a direct challenge to Caesar, the Senate, and all the principalities and powers of the Roman Empire. In the context of the kind of imperial decrees common in the Roman world, Mark is introducing his Gospel something like this: "The beginning of the real gospel of Jesus the King, the true Son of God." Mark's Gospel will not be a benign meditation on private spirituality, but a subversive political challenge to the principalities and powers. Mark launches immediately into Jesus' proclamation of the arrival of a new and alternative political order that he calls the kingdom of God.

Lord Jesus, help us to hear your proclamation of the kingdom of God as radical and revolutionary; help us,

Lord, to rethink everything and believe this good news. Amen.

Third Week of Advent

Saturday

Matthew 1:1–17

The Genealogy of Jesus

I have two dear Russian friends who grew up in the Soviet Union during the era of Communism and its official atheism. In a most remarkable way they became Christians while students in art school. Upon their conversion they were given a Bible by an American tourist—a Gideon pocket New Testament in King James English. But neither of them spoke a word of English. So they bought a Russian-English dictionary and set about the laborious task of translating the Gospel from English to Russian word for word, from Latin script to Cyrillic script. I can scarcely imagine what a daunting undertaking this must have been. When they first told me this story, I said, "The beginning of the New Testament is a genealogy. Did that disappoint you?" They replied, "No, it excited us! We didn't know what it meant but we knew it was important." And that's our reading today—the genealogy of Jesus. Perhaps we can say with my friends

Igor and Dmitri, even if we don't know exactly what it means, we know it's important.

And it is important—it's important to realize that Jesus of Nazareth enters our world with a family history. The Son of God did not enter the human story by swooping down from heaven in a golden chariot but was born with a traceable patrilineal genealogy (even if his humanity was entirely derived from his mother). In Jesus of Nazareth God joins the human story with all of its long history. The Irish theologian and philosopher Herbert McCabe says it like this: "The story of Jesus is nothing other than the triune life of God projected onto our history, or enacted sacramentally in our history, so that it becomes story." To belong to human history is to have the backstory of a genealogy, and that's what we find in these first verses of the New Testament.

Matthew opens his gospel by first giving us a summary of Jesus' genealogy: "The son of David, the Son of Abraham." Who is Jesus? He is the son of David and heir to an eternal throne; he is the seed of Abraham destined to bless all the families of the earth. Jesus is how God keeps his covenant promises to Abraham and David. The story of Jesus doesn't begin in Matthew, rather it is a continuation of a story that began in Genesis.

At the end of the genealogy Matthew points out that Jesus is the culmination of three sets of fourteen generations. (This is why in the Church of the Nativity in Bethlehem the traditional spot of Jesus' birth is marked by a fourteen-point silver star.) But another way of saying this is that Jesus is born at the conclusion of six sets of seven generations. Thus with the coming of Jesus we enter the seventh set of generations—an auspicious thing indeed. In a clever and cryptic way Matthew is alerting the careful reader that something divine and deeply significant has begun with the birth of Jesus. Amen! The anticipated Christ has been born!

O God, in Christ you have joined your story with our story, that the human story might become one of salvation. We thank you and praise you for this holy mystery. Amen.

FOURTH WEEK OF ADVENT
SUNDAY

Matthew 1:18–25
Mary and Joseph

In 735 BC the prophet Isaiah told King Ahaz that "the young woman shall conceive and bear a son, and shall call his name Immanuel"—a prophecy that in one sense was fulfilled with the birth of Hezekiah. But the Septuagint (the 3rd century BC Greek translation of the Hebrew Bible) says, "the virgin shall conceive," and this is where we find the deeper mystery and the greater prophecy. Indeed, as we confess in the Apostles' Creed, Jesus Christ "was conceived by the power of the Holy Spirit and born of the Virgin Mary." We'll look at the mystery of the Theotokos on Tuesday when we read Luke's account of the Annunciation, but today I want to focus our attention on one of the most overlooked figures in the life of Jesus: Joseph.

Joseph was Mary's fiancé (Matthew uses the word husband), when it was discovered that Mary was pregnant before they had been together. Such an occurrence is scandalous today, but in a 1st century Jewish society it was unimaginably so! Joseph decides to annul their betrothal, but because he is a righteous man he intends to do as discreetly as possible and protect Mary from public shame. Joseph is hurt, but he has no desire to hurt Mary. Though Joseph will not be Mary's husband, he will remain her protector. This tells us a lot about Joseph's character. Having demonstrated that he has the depth of virtue to serve as the surrogate father for the Son of God, an angel explains to Joseph that the child has been conceived by the Holy Spirit and that indeed a virgin will bear a son.

We don't know very much about Joseph, or at least not as much as we would like. We know that though he descended from the royal line of David, he was a humble carpenter plying his trade in an obscure Galilean village. But we never hear any direct words from Joseph. He is one of those quiet men whose deep goodness is found in what they do, not in what they say. Joseph isn't a prophet or a preacher; he's a protector and provider.

The other thing we can deduce from the life of Joseph is that he taught Jesus his building trade. In the Gospels Jesus is called both "the carpenter" and "the carpenter's son." It's fascinating to think of how the architect of the universe became an apprentice to a humble carpenter. The one who is the Word of God and spoke the cosmos into existence also became one who worked with his hands in a construction trade. Joseph taught the one who is the Wisdom of God.

By the time Jesus begins his public ministry it appears that Joseph has died. Was this perhaps Jesus' first experience with deep grief? Was the Man of Sorrows' first sorrow the death of his father? To imagine a young Jesus weeping at Joseph's burial is a holy thing and hints at the great depth of the mystery of the Incarnation.

O God, we thank you for the good, quiet Josephs whom you have placed in our lives. Help us to recognize and appreciate what a great gift they are. Amen.

Fourth Week of Advent
Monday

Luke 1:5–24
Zechariah and Elizabeth

Today we move to Luke's Gospel and we will be with the third Gospel for eleven days—the Evangelist who gives us more Advent and Christmas themes than any other. After his preliminary dedication to Theophilus, Luke begins his Gospel with these words: "In the days of King Herod." Luke's story is set during the dark days when Judea was occupied by Rome and their king was a client of Caesar. Herod the Great (72–4 BC) was installed as the King of Judea by the Roman Senate in 37 BC as a reward for military service on behalf of the empire. Herod was a daring general and a great builder, but he was also a corrupt and paranoid king capable of astonishing cruelty. After waiting so long for a king, Herod was certainly not the righteous king the pious of Israel had been praying for. As Luke's story opens Herod has reigned for some thirty years, his dynasty is in place, and the hope for a messianic king seemed farther away than ever.

At the same time there lived in the hill country of Judea a humble priest and his wife—Zechariah and Elizabeth. They were blameless, but blamelessness had not led to blessedness, for Elizabeth was barren. They had prayed for a child for decades, but no child had come, and now they were getting on in years. Of course by this point in the Bible we see this as the foreshadowing of a special birth—barren women giving birth to great sons is a common biblical motif seen in Sarah, Rebekah, Rachel, Hannah, and the wife of Manoah. And sure enough, when Zechariah is chosen by lot to offer incense in the Temple—a once in a lifetime opportunity—he encounters the angel Gabriel who tells him that his wife will bear a son, his name is to be called John, and he will prepare the people for the coming of Messiah.

Gabriel began his announcement to Zechariah by saying, "Do not be afraid." Angels always say "fear not" because this is what heaven has to say to earth. Then the angel says, "Your prayer has been heard." Zechariah and Elizabeth had been praying for a child for a long time, perhaps for as long as Herod had been king. The answer to their prayer had been delayed so that God can give them more than a child—God will give them the forerunner of Messiah! Sometimes the answer to our prayers is delayed so that God can answer them in a way greater than we could ever imagine.

Among the instructions given to Zechariah was that John was to drink no wine. John the Baptist drinks no wine because he's not the one who brings the party, he only prepares the way. The party begins when Jesus turns the water to wine at the wedding feast in Cana. John is Advent; Jesus is Christmas.

O God, help us to hear the heavenly announcement to fear not, and help us to persevere in prayer even when the answer is delayed. We thank you that it is your good pleasure to do exceedingly abundantly above and beyond all that we can ask or think. Amen.

FOURTH WEEK OF ADVENT

TUESDAY

Luke 1:26–38
The Annunciation

It was through a young and poor Jewish maiden named Miriam (Mary) living in the backwater Galilean village of Nazareth during the Roman occupation of the first century that the Eternal Logos, the Word of God, took on flesh and became the God-Man. In Christian theology we call this event the Incarnation and Mary is known as the Theotokos—the God-bearer. The Incarnation of Christ through the Theotokos is one of the most sacred confessions and sublime mysteries of Christian faith. It's the story of how through the cooperation of the Virgin Mary and the Holy Spirit the Divine-Eternal became an enfleshed human. And it begins with the Annunciation—the Announcement.

In the sixth month of her relative Elizabeth's pregnancy, the angel Gabriel came to Nazareth to tell an engaged, but not yet married, virgin that she will conceive and give birth to a son named Jesus and that he will be the long-awaited Messiah whose kingdom will have no end. When Mary questioned the angel saying, "How can this be? I do not know a man?", the angel simply responded, "The Holy Spirit." This is the enduring pattern by which God brings redemptive newness into the world. How? *The Holy Spirit.*

Mary as the mother of Christ is the entirely unique Theotokos. But on another level Mary is the universal archetype for all who yield to the Holy Spirit and say with the Virgin, "Here am I, the servant of the Lord; let it be unto me according to your word." As we learn to say yes to the Holy Spirit, we become a lesser theotokos through whom God can bring something holy into the world.

As I read Luke's account of the Annunciation I'm struck by the profusion of names. In this short story no less than nine names appear—the names of six people, two places, and one angel. The story of the Annunciation with its many names can be summed up like this.

> The angel **Gabriel** came to **Nazareth** in **Galilee** to tell **Mary**, the fiancé of **Joseph** and relative of **Elizabeth** that she

will give birth to a son named **Jesus**, who be the heir of **David** and will reign over the house of **Jacob**.

The abundance of names that appear in the Annunciation is a reminder that salvation is not abstract or theoretical but *historical*. Christianity is not a religion based in esoteric ideas but in historical events. To preach the gospel is not to present ideas, but to tell a story; our Christian faith has a narrative arc to it. So in the Apostles' Creed we confess, "I believe in Jesus Christ, God's only Son; he was conceived by the power of the Holy Spirit and born of the Virgin Mary." Ultimately Christianity is a confession, not an explanation. We will explain what we can, but we will always confess more than we can explain. Today we confess the sacred mystery of the virgin birth.

O God, draw us beyond the sterile world of abstract ideas into the enchanted world of the sacred gospel story—a story that proclaims that by the Holy Spirit a virgin girl became the Mother of God. Amen.

FOURTH WEEK OF ADVENT

WEDNESDAY

Luke 1:39–45

Mary and Elizabeth

What news would make you literally leap for joy? What would it take for you to jump up and down and throw your hat in the air? It's what people did at the end of WWII and at the fall of the Berlin Wall. It's what you might do if you won the lottery or found out that you're cancer-free. When war ends and tyranny topples, when prosperity comes and sickness goes, it's the kind of good news that elicits exuberant celebration. And it's this kind of good news that Mary and Elizabeth celebrate together. It's the good news that the kingdom of God is at last breaking into a world dominated by proud and brutal tyrants.

Elizabeth had endured long years of heartbreaking infertility—a sorrow made worse by the undeserved stigma associated with barrenness in ancient societies. Elizabeth describes her experience of childlessness as "the disgrace I have endured among my people." (Luke 1:25) But now she is six months pregnant with a child who will be known to history as John the Baptist. Mary is a much younger relative of Elizabeth and is carrying in her womb the Son of God conceived by the Holy Spirit. We can assume that the only other person aware of Mary's miraculous pregnancy is her fiancé Joseph—and an angel had to explain the nature of her pregnancy to him. We can also imagine that Mary longed for a trusted friend in whom she could confide, and this is why she made the long journey into the hill country of Judea to be with her older relative Elizabeth. As it turns out both of these women have quite a story to tell.

When Mary arrives at the home of Zechariah and greets her relative with the customary, *Shalom*, Elizabeth responds with an astounding prophetic utterance: "Blessed are you among women, and blessed is the fruit of your womb! Why am I so honored that the mother of my Lord should come to visit me?" And at that moment John the Baptist in the womb of his mother began to leap for joy. What a beautiful picture of irrepressible joy. The anticipation of the coming of the kingdom of God is marked by unbridled elation. Truly the kingdom of God is "righteousness and peace and joy in the Holy Spirit." (Romans 14:17)

As we look at this story we should notice the deep prophetic symbolism that occurs when these two mothers-to-be meet. A woman almost too old to have a child will give birth to a son who will close out an old age, and a woman almost too young to have a child will give birth to a son who will inaugurate a new age. In this we see the recurring biblical pattern first set forth in Genesis: "The older will serve the younger." (Genesis 25:23) Though we read about John the Baptist in the New Testament, theologically it is John the Baptist as the second coming of Elijah who closes out the Old Testament. Indeed, all newness begins with Christ. Let us leap for joy!

O God, we thank you that in Christ all things are made new, and that in this newness we find the joy of heaven arriving on earth. Help us today to enter into that joy. Amen.

Fourth Week of Advent
Thursday

Luke 1:46–55
The Magnificat

Our reading today is a song that has become one of the most frequently prayed passages of Scripture in Christianity. I chant this song every morning during Advent and Christmas, and it's always in my evening liturgy of prayer. The Song of Mary is most commonly known as the Magnificat (Latin for "magnifies"). As significant as Mary is in the Christian story, we only hear her speak four times: to the angel at the Annunciation, to Jesus at age twelve in the Temple, to Jesus at the wedding feast in Cana, and here in the Magnificat. The Magnificat is certainly a hymn of praise, but it's also a subversive revolutionary anthem.

The first thing to notice about the Magnificat is that it is an adaptation of Hannah's song (1 Samuel 2:1–10). Hannah became the mother of the prophet Samuel. She had been barren and was bitterly tormented by her husband's second wife, but Hannah conceived after making a vow to dedicate her firstborn son to the Lord. Her song is a hymn of gratitude and triumph that speaks of how God intervenes on behalf of the unfortunate. Part of Hannah's song goes like this:

> He raises the poor from the dust,
> He lifts the needy from the ash heap,
> He makes them sit with princes.

In comparing the songs of Hannah and Mary we see how the New Testament is dependent upon the First Testament. And what stands out about both songs is how revolutionary they are. Think of how subversive these words were in the context of Mary's time—the time of King Herod.

> He has brought down the powerful from
>   their thrones,
> And lifted up the lowly;
> He has filled the hungry with good
>   things,
> And the rich he has sent away empty.

Mary's Magnificat anticipates what will happen when her son grows up and begins to proclaim the good news of the kingdom. It will be welcomed by the poor, the sick, the downcast and outcast who are open to Jesus' message while the rich and powerful will mostly resist it. What we should learn from the Magnificat is that the grace of God flows downhill toward the lowly places in our lives where we are humble, weak, and poor. There may be places in your life where you are strong, successful, and rich. And this can be a blessing. But be careful and always remember that grace flows downhill.

In our contemporary context we need a Christianity formed by the Magnificat. In the American superpower we are typically inclined toward ideologies of success and anthems of strength. But the grace of God does not run uphill toward the pinnacles of success and strength, it rolls downhill toward the low places of humility and trust. Advent is not just about waiting, but about waiting in the right place. The right place to wait for the grace of God is the lowly ash heap of your barrenness and brokenness. This is where the grace of God will appear.

O God, help us to identify the ash heap of barrenness and brokenness in our lives and to wait there for your grace to come lift us up. Most merciful God, we trust not in our strength, but in your grace. Amen.

FOURTH WEEK OF ADVENT
FRIDAY

Luke 1:57–66

The Birth of John the Baptist

First the country priest encountered an angel while offering incense in the Temple. Then his long-barren wife was found to be with child. Now upon the birth of the child, and after nine months of enforced silence, the mute priest speaks for the first time. It's clear that the birth of this child named John is auspicious. It's easy to understand why the friends and neighbors of Zechariah and Elizabeth wondered, "What then will this child become?" Let's jump ahead about thirty years and try to answer their question.

What John did *not* become is what most people would have been expected—he did not become a priest like his father. Instead of following Zechariah into the priesthood, John retreated into the wilderness. Luke says it like this, "The child grew and became strong in spirit, and was in the wilderness until the day he publicly appeared to Israel." (Luke 1:80) At some point, maybe in his teen years, John left his home and began to live in the rugged Judean wilderness. Perhaps his elderly parents were already dead by then. Did John live among the Essenes—the separatist apocalyptic community near the Dead Sea at Qumran, the people who produced the Dead Sea Scrolls? Of course, we don't know. What we know is what Luke tells us: that John lived in the wilderness becoming spiritually strong until he began to preach and baptize at the Jordan River in the fifteenth year of the reign of Emperor Tiberius (AD 28).

John was the prophet who, as the angel Gabriel told Zechariah, would "come in the spirit and power of Elijah." (Luke 1:17) But John was more than a prophet, he was the forerunner foretold by Isaiah and Malachi. It was his prophetic task to make ready a people prepared for the Lord. John did this by preaching a message of repentance and baptizing the penitent. His sermons were filled with themes of justice—calling the rich to share their wealth and the police to stop employing violent tactics of intimidation. (See Luke 3:10–14) John's preaching was wildly popular with the masses and drew huge crowds from Jerusalem. But, predictably, John's ministry had little or no effect on the Temple establishment.

The apex of John's meteoric ministry was to baptize Jesus. Once that was accomplished, the crowds began to leave John and follow Jesus instead. John the Baptist took his diminished role with humility and grace, telling his disciples, "He must increase, but I must decrease." (John 3:30) A few months after he had baptized Jesus, John was arrested by Herod, and not long after that he was executed. Jesus himself delivered John's eulogy in advance, saying, "Among those born of women no one is greater than John; yet the least in the kingdom of God is greater than he." (Luke 7:28) Jesus was indicating that John was the culmination of an epoch begun with Abraham, but now a new epoch was dawning with the coming of the Son of Man.

O God, help us to follow in the footsteps of the prophetic forerunner, John, by continually saying of our Lord Jesus Christ: He must increase, but I must decrease. Amen.

Fourth Week of Advent
Saturday

Luke 1:67–79
The Song of Zechariah

Advent and Christmas are seasons of song—without our carols it just wouldn't be Christmas. Songs are poetry set to music, and poetry is how we express the ineffable. The precision of prose has its place, but it cannot properly speak of the transcendent. Language that aspires to describe the divine is best done as poetry. By poetry I don't necessarily mean rhyming verse, but language that prioritizes form over function, beauty over utility, passion over pragmatism. The power of poetry to speak of the divine is why Genesis opens with poetry, why the Hebrew prophets were mostly poets, why the psalms are *all* poetry, and why so much of the best of the New Testament is poetic: The Beatitudes, the prologue to John's Gospel, Paul's ode to love that is I Corinthians 13, and the majestic anthems of praise found in Revelation.

On Thursday we looked at Mary's revolutionary song, the Magnificat. Next week we will look at Simeon's swan song. But today we have Zechariah's song before us—a song composed at the birth of his son, John the Baptist. Zechariah's prophetic song might be described as a poetic meditation on salvation. Here are some selected lines from Zechariah's song as translated by the New Testament scholar N.T. Wright.

> Blessed be the Lord, Israel's God!
> He's come to his people and bought them
>   their freedom.
> Salvation from our enemies, rescue from
>   hatred,
> to give us deliverance from fear and from
>   foes,
> letting his people know of salvation,
> through the forgiveness of all their sins.
> The heart of our God is full of mercy,
> that's why his daylight has dawned from
>   on high,
> bringing light to the dark, as we sat in
>   death's shadow,
> guiding our feet in the path of peace.

What a beautiful song of salvation! Zechariah's poem says that through Messiah we are saved from enemies and hate, fear and foes, placing our feet on the path of peace. And isn't that all we really want—to be set free from fear and to walk in peace? But we must not make the mistake of thinking that this salvation can come by the way of the world. A world under the sway of the wicked one says we're saved from our enemies by destroying our enemies; that we're saved from those who hate us by hating them even more; that we're saved by fear by placing the highest priority on security; that we can only walk in peace when we have eliminated every possible threat. Of course this is nothing more than salvation according to Caesar. When the Messiah whose way is prepared by Zechariah's son appears, he won't save Israel by being more Caesar than Caesar. Messiah won't play the devil's game of trying to conquer fear by fear, hate by hate, violence by violence. Messiah will be the savior who guides our feet into the way of peace—the blessed paths of God's shalom.

O God, we praise you for the salvation you have sent into the world through your Son our savior, Jesus

Christ. Guide our feet, we pray, into the paths of shalom as we seek to follow the Prince of Peace. Amen.

CHRISTMAS EVE
DECEMBER 24

Luke 2:1–20
The Christmas Story

It's Christmas Eve, the holiest night of the year, the night when the stores finally close and even commerce bows its knee to Christ. As a child I delighted in Christmas morning, as every child does, but I think I enjoyed Christmas Eve more. Christmas Eve in my home had a mysterious quality to it that appealed to my young imagination. Candles were lit, special treats were served, and then we would sit around the tree where my dad would read two stories: The Christmas story from Luke and *The Night Before Christmas*. As the children got older, it was a rite of passage to memorize Luke 2:1–20 in the King James Version and then recite it on Christmas Eve. To this day I only want to hear the Christmas story in King James.

One of the greatest gifts we can provide for children is to give them a Christmas tradition that, along with Santa, the tree, the presents, and all the rest, also has a memorable telling of the story of the babe born in Bethlehem. In *The Everlasting Man*, G.K. Chesterton says that anyone "whose childhood has known a real Christmas has ever afterwards an association in his mind between two ideas that most of mankind must regard as remote from each other; the idea of a baby and the idea of unknown strength that sustains the stars. His instincts and imagination can still connect them." The story of the birth in the city of David of a savior who is Christ the Lord, captured my imagination as a child, and, lo, these many years later it still does.

On Christmas Eve I don't want to read any Lukan commentaries; I don't want any learned examinations of the taxation policies implemented by Caesar Augustus; I don't want any historical-critical investigations into the Syrian governorship of Cyrenius; I just want to hear the story. I want to hear about a woman great with child who traveled with her betrothed from Nazareth to Bethlehem, how there was no room in the inn, so the babe was born among the beasts. I want to hear about shepherds keeping watch over their flocks by night and how they were sore afraid when the angel appeared. I want to hear how the shepherds came with haste and found Mary and Joseph and the babe lying in a manger. I just want to hear the Christmas story! Because, after all, that's what the gospel is—the story of Jesus. It's not a formula or a plan; it's a sacred story that connects the idea of a baby with the unknown strength that sustains the stars.

So perhaps at the end of this holy day you can find a quiet moment to light a candle, read Luke's Christmas story, and allow your imagination to transport you to a stable in Bethlehem two thousand years ago where there is a babe wrapped in swaddling clothes, lying in a manger. Then, like Mary, you can keep all these things and ponder them in your heart.

O God, we stand in awe of the greatest story ever told; the gospel story of how the Creator became creature, of how the Word became flesh, how Omnipotence became a newborn baby. We praise you for the mystery and majesty of the story we celebrate with Christmas. Amen.

CHRISTMAS DAY
DECEMBER 25

Luke 2:8–14
The Christmas Angels

Merry Christmas! The Advent wait is over and Christ is born! The first to know of Messiah's birth were Bethlehem shepherds who heard the news from an angel: "Fear not! For behold, I bring you good tidings of great joy, which shall be to all people. For unto you is born this day in the city of David a Savior, which is Christ the Lord." Suddenly a multitude of angels appeared to sing the first Christmas carol: "Glory to God in the highest, and on earth peace, good will toward men."

Angels are abundant in the Christmas story. Angels deliver prenatal announcements to Zechariah and Mary. Angels appear to Joseph no less than three times. An angel announces the birth of Christ to startled shepherds. A heavenly choir of angels sing in praise of good will and peace on earth. I like to contemplate angels, and whereas I refrain from claiming any definite knowledge about the nature of angels, I believe I can say that the angelic is the heavenly assistance that traverses the fissure between the spiritual and the material worlds. In the Christmas story angels are emissaries of grace and good will who lend assistance in critical moments. We humans live our lives on earth suspended between heaven and hell, life and death, good and evil, but we are not left to fend for ourselves—God sends help from heaven. Perhaps this is the simplest way to understand the angelic: it is help from heaven. In our Advent journey we've already seen a good deal of angelic help. An angel helps Zechariah and Elizabeth prepare for the birth and mission of their long-awaited son. An angel helps the Virgin Mary accept the call to become the mother of God's son. An angel helps Joseph understand the nature of Mary's pregnancy.

In these stories the angels visibly appear as they render their assistance. And though most of us have never met Gabriel, that doesn't mean we haven't been aided by heaven's help. How many times have we been helped to understand something, to prepare for something, been protected or prompted to take the right course, all by some vaguely sensed spiritual nudge? Yes, angels are all around us!

The Christmas angels who appeared to the shepherds sang of peace on earth and good will toward men. Heaven is always seeking to pull us toward peace and good will, while hell seeks to drag us toward war and malice. If we cooperate with hate and ill-will we are left bereft of heaven's aid and the angels sing their song in vain. But on Christmas Day we are reminded of the better way—the way of heaven, the way of the angels, the way of God, the way of the Prince of Peace. So on this Christmas Day allow the angels' song to lift your heart away from a world of strife and into the celestial peace and joy that comes from heaven. Merry Christmas!

O God, on this most joyful day we thank you for the help you send from heaven on the wings of angels; but even more we praise you for the salvation you have sent to earth through your Son Jesus Christ. Today may our feast and celebration be unto your glory. Amen.

SECOND DAY OF CHRISTMAS
DECEMBER 26

Luke 2:22–24
The Presentation of Jesus

Merry Christmas! Yes, it's still Christmas. In the secular calendar Christmas is over and done with on December 25 and the next "holy day" is New Year's Eve. But in the sacred calendar—the tradition that gave us Christmas in the first place—the celebration of the birth of Christ is a twelve-day feast. In modernity the speed of life becomes ever faster and more frenetic, and this contributes to a shallowness of soul that we experience as disenchantment. The sacred calendar, on the other hand, comes from a slower and more contemplative time. Our premodern forebearers of the faith knew that the birth of Christ was worthy of a twelve-day feast. So I urge you to resist the secular impulse to put Christmas behind and rush toward the new year. Slow down and settle deeply into Christmas wonder. Advent is four weeks of waiting, but now that the waiting is over let us not be in a hurry to leave what we've been waiting for. Let's look into the mystery and majesty of the birth of the Son of God for twelve full days.

Our reading from Luke's Gospel recounts an event that occurred forty days after the birth of Jesus. According to the Torah every firstborn male of man and beast was holy to the Lord. Clean animals were to be offered to God upon the altar, and sons were to be presented to God and redeemed with the requisite sacrifice on their behalf. We might think of this as the "law of first things." In dedicating the first things to God the worshiper is acknowledging God's ownership of all things. This is the spiritual philosophy of the tithe. It's also what is reflected in the passage on material possessions in the Sermon on the Mount when Jesus says, "Seek first the kingdom of God and his justice, and all these things shall be added unto you." (Matthew 6:33)

In the Torah the Hebrew people were instructed to redeem firstborn sons with the sacrifice of a lamb, but the poor were allowed to offer two pigeons or turtledoves as an inexpensive substitute. That Mary and Joseph offered birds and not a lamb at the dedication of Jesus indicates that they were situated among the ranks of the

126

poor. This is something we should ponder. The King of Kings was not born in a palace but in a stable; the Lord of Lords did not live among the elite but with the unfortunate. Jesus was born into a family of poor and pious Jews who struggled to survive under the crushing weight of Roman occupation. Jesus' formative years were lived among a people who were rich in faith and tradition but poor in material possessions. The concern for the poor that Jesus exhibited in his ministry years came from both his divine nature and his human experience. On the second day of Christmas, consider this Christ mystery: Though he was rich, for our sake he became poor, that through his poverty we might become rich. (2 Corinthians 8:9)

Lord Jesus, as we continue to celebrate your birth, help us to seek first your kingdom, and to ever remember that when you came among us you were found not with the privileged but with the poor. Amen.

THIRD DAY OF CHRISTMAS
DECEMBER 27

Luke 2:25–35
Simeon

When we think of Jerusalem in the time of Jesus we may tend to think of the antagonists in the gospel story—the depraved King Herod, the corrupt High Priest Caiaphas, the hypocritical Sadducees, the self-righteous Pharisees. But this doesn't tell the whole story; there were also the righteous and devout, and among these pious people was an old man named Simeon. Simeon was aware of the political and religious corruption that was all around him, but he had not become cynical, because he was waiting and looking for the "Consolation of Israel"—a poetic title for the Messiah. And though Simon had been waiting his whole life for this consolation and was now an old man, he held on to a revelation from the Holy Spirit that he would not see death until he had seen the Lord's Messiah. This was the living hope that prevented Simeon from becoming a bitter old man.

One day the Spirit prompted Simeon to go to the Temple, and there he saw a young couple performing the rites of dedication for their infant son. The Spirit revealed to Simeon that the child being dedicated was the long-awaited Messiah! What happens next is a very tender scene. Simeon approached the couple, took Jesus gently in his arms, and began to praise God in song—we might call it Simeon's swan song.

> Lord, you now have set your servant free
> to go in peace as you have promised;
> For these eyes of mine have seen the Savior,
> Whom you have prepared for all the world to see:
> A Light to enlighten the nations,
> and the glory of your people Israel.

Having seen the salvation of Israel, Simeon can now die in peace. Of course he has no real idea how this baby will bring salvation to Israel, but for Simeon it is enough to know he has held salvation in his arms. Simeon then blessed Mary and Joseph and spoke mysteriously about the destiny of the child, about a great struggle, and of a sorrow that would pierce Mary's soul.

We cannot hope for ourselves or for those whom we love to go through life without struggle, pain, and sorrow. No one gets through life unscarred—the sword of sorrow pierces every heart. If in our fear we cling to a false hope of avoiding all pain we only make the pain worse when it inevitably comes. Our hope is not in the avoidance of all pain but in in the Consolation of Israel who can and will redeem all things in his salvation. It's as we hold that promise close to our hearts like Simeon holding the infant Christ that we are kept in perfect peace. We may not know how all things will be redeemed, how every tear will be wiped away, but for now it is enough to know that it is Jesus Christ who is the Consolation of the world.

Lord Jesus, as we look upon you and know that you are the Lord's salvation, may the peace that Simeon knew enter our hearts and calm our fears. Amen.

FOURTH DAY OF CHRISTMAS
DECEMBER 28

Luke 2:36–38
Anna

Yesterday we saw Simeon's prophetic encounter with the holy family, and today we meet another aged prophet in the Christmas story—Anna, the daughter of Phanuel. Anna was what later Christian tradition would call an anchorite—a person who attaches themselves to a church and never leaves, living an ascetic life of prayer. The most famous anchorite in Christian history is Julian of Norwich (1343–1416) who lived the final decades of her life in a cell in St. Julian's Church in Norwich, England. Her book *Revelations of Divine Love* is the most important of all medieval mystical texts. Like Mother Julian, Anna never left the Temple, worshiping there day and night.

We can make some educated guesses about Anna's life from hints left by Luke. She was eighty-four years of age and was widowed after seven years of marriage. This would mean that Anna was widowed around the same time that the famous Roman general Pompey conquered Jerusalem. Under General Pompey the Roman army besieged Jerusalem for three months before finally breaking through the defenses and entering the city. Twelve thousand Jewish defenders made their final stand on the Temple Mount where they were slain by the Romans. Following the slaughter Pompey waded through the carnage and entered the Holy of Holies—an unspeakable sacrilege. The holy city of Jerusalem was now subject to pagan Roman rule. Was Anna's husband among the twelve thousand Jewish defenders slain by Pompey? In her sorrow did she enter the Temple, never again to leave? Luke may hint at this.

Anna was not only a proto-anchorite, she was also a prophet. When she saw the infant Jesus in the Temple she began to praise God and prophesy about the child to all who were longing for the redemption of Jerusalem. Anna had seen much sorrow and suffering in her long life, but now she found reason to rejoice in the birth of a child. At eighty-four Anna knew she would not live to see how the child would bring salvation to Jerusalem, but she had seen the child and she now had hope.

Simeon and Anna. An old man and an old woman in the Temple on the day that Jesus was dedicated. These two old prophets spoke of the infant Jesus as salvation and redemption. Indeed, Jesus will save both Simeon and Anna, but neither of them know how—in fact, neither of them really know what salvation truly is. But this is not a problem. Salvation is not based on theological acumen; salvation is based entirely on trust. Salvation is not found in believing the right *things*, but in trusting the right *person*. What matters is not if Simeon and Anna know the "plan of salvation" (they don't), but that they know the right person. What they know is that however salvation comes, it will come through the little baby that a Galilean couple are dedicating in the Temple. As the old saying goes, it's not what you know but who you know.

Lord Jesus, we have come to know and believe that you are the salvation of God. We may not know how salvation will come and what it will fully look like but, Jesus, we know you. We confess that you are the Savior of the world. Amen.

FIFTH DAY OF CHRISTMAS
DECEMBER 29

John 1:1–5
The Eternal Logos

For the next three days, the final three days of the year, we will be in the poetic prologue to John's Gospel—my favorite passage of Scripture in the entire Bible. The theopoetic opening to the Fourth Gospel is a creative synthesis of Hebrew revelation and Greek wisdom—a synthesis that describes Christianity theology itself. In a daring move John begins his Gospel with an "In the beginning" echo of Genesis 1:1. John writes that in the beginning was the Word—the Eternal Logos, the Infinite Idea, the Logic of Love, the Divine Wisdom. This Logos is the wisdom by which God founded the earth and established the heavens (Proverbs 3:19). The Logos is the creative Word of God in the economy of the Trinity—and this Word is Christ. Jesus Christ as the Word of God is both the creator and the sustainer of creation—as the

Apostle Paul says, "In him all things hold together" (Colossians 2:17).

A century ago, in the aftermath of a global war and a global pandemic, the Irish poet William Butler Yeats wrote, "things fall apart, the center cannot hold." In the context of the time Yeats' poem (The Second Coming) had a prophetic truth to it. But the greater truth is that there is a center that holds—the Eternal Logos that sustains all things and which cannot be overcome by the chaotic darkness of evil. Every star and every galaxy, every blade of grass and every grain of sand continues to exist because they are sustained by the Eternal Word of God.

As Christians, when we think of the Word of God our first thought should be of Jesus Christ, not the Bible. Yes, we can speak of the Bible as the word of God, but only in a secondary sense. The true Word of God is that to which the Bible testifies: Jesus Christ. Jesus is the full and perfect Word of God in a way the Bible never can be. In his Unspoken Sermons George MacDonald writes,

> Sad, indeed, would the matter be, if the Bible had told us everything God meant us to believe. But herein is the Bible greatly wronged. It nowhere lays claim to

be regarded as the Word, the Way, the Truth. The Bible leads us to Jesus, the inexhaustible, the ever unfolding revelation of God. It is Christ "in whom are hid all the treasures of wisdom and knowledge," not the Bible, save as leading to him.

We believe in the infallible, inerrant Word of God...and his name is Jesus! We cherish the inspired text that is the Bible because it infallibly points us to Jesus. We are not called to believe in the Bible so much as we are called to believe in the one to whom the Bible testifies. In debate with his religious opponents, Jesus said it like this:

> You search the Scriptures because you think that in them you have eternal life; and it is they that testify of me. Yet you refuse to come to me that you may have life. (John 5:39–40)

Lord Jesus, you are the true Word of God, the Logos that enlightens us, the living Word that gives us life.

We come to you that we might live in the light of your saving word. Amen.

SIXTH DAY OF
CHRISTMAS
DECEMBER 30

John 1:6–13, 15
The True Light

In the dark world of idolatry all illumination is precious. The ancient Hebrews had the moonlight of the Law and the starry constellations of the Prophets by which they could navigate through the shadows of night on their journey toward truth. The Gentiles had the flickering candles of nature's witness and Greek wisdom by which they could grope for God. (Acts 17:27) Moonlight, starlight, and candlelight are faint illuminations in the darkness of night. But when the sun rises the darkness is altogether dispelled—the night is done, the day has dawned. The prophet Malachi spoke of the coming of Messiah as the sun of righteousness that will rise with healing in its wings. (Malachi 4:2) And John the Evangelist tells us that the light from the life of Jesus

Christ is the illumination of true enlightenment. In the life of Jesus Christ, we receive the dual enlightenment revealing who God is and how to be human.

Like the cock that crows to herald the sunrise, John the Baptist was the herald to announce the coming of the True Light. John was not the Light, he was the witness sent to testify to the Light. And the relationship of John the Baptist to Jesus Christ is analogous to the relationship of the Bible to the Christ as the true Word of God. John is to Jesus what the Bible is to Jesus. Think of it like this:

> There was a book sent from God whose name was Bible. It came as a witness to testify to the Light, so that all might believe through it. The Bible itself was not the Light, but it came to bear witness to the Light. The True Light, which enlightens everyone, was coming into the world. The Bible testified to him and cried out, "This is he of whom I said, 'He who comes after me ranks ahead of me because he was before me.'"

Indeed, what is true of John the Baptist is also true of the Bible. Jesus came after John and the Bible but ranks ahead of John and the Bible because as the Eternal Logos he was before them both. The true witness of the Bible is to point us to the True Light that is Jesus Christ. Our question is not, can we find it in the Bible; the question is, can we find it in the life of Jesus Christ. We can find many things in the Bible that we cannot find in Christ. Wars of conquest, ethnic cleansing, the institution of slavery, capital punishment, and women held as property are all things present in the Bible but absent in Jesus. If we go to the Bible to find the light of truth, the Bible will faithfully point us to the True Light who is Jesus Christ. Some parts of the Bible belong to a dim archaic past, but the Light of Christ never dims. The light of Christ is the true enlightenment.

Lord Jesus, we have received the witness of Scripture and have come to know that you are the True Light. May your light so shine upon us that we may ever walk in the paths of truth. Amen.

SEVENTH DAY OF CHRISTMAS

DECEMBER 31

John 1:14–18
The Word Made Flesh

On this seventh day of Christmas we arrive at the merriest of Christmas revelations—the Word made flesh! The Eternal Logos, the Infinite Idea, the Logic of Love, the Divine Wisdom, God's Understanding of God's Self, assumed human nature to heal human nature. The moment the Word became flesh the salvation of humanity was guaranteed. All the events of God's salvation would have to run their course through time, from incarnation to crucifixion to resurrection, but the salvific end was always inevitable. When the Word was made flesh, the world was saved.

The apostles of Christ saw, and through their witness we too have seen, the beauty of the Father fully displayed in the life of Jesus Christ—a life overflowing with grace and truth. The grace and truth of God that

Moses and the Prophets could never fully embody is fully found in the Word made flesh. From the infinite fullness of God there is an endless flow of grace into humanity. Imagine an hourglass with its two spheres and the connecting point where the sand flows from the upper sphere into the lower. Now imagine an upper sphere that is infinite. That's what we find in the Word made flesh. Jesus became the point that connects the infinite grace of God with the finite deficiency of humanity. This is salvation. This is why we say, *Merry Christmas!*

John concludes his poetic prologue by insisting that no one has ever seen God—it is God the Son who is near the Father's heart who has made God known. This is a daring statement from John. We might protest and point out that Abraham saw God and had a meal with him under the oaks of Mamre; Jacob saw God with angels ascending and descending on the ladder at Bethel; Moses saw God face to face on Mount Sinai and his face shone from the encounter; the seventy elders of Israel went on to Mount Sinai and saw God as they ate and drank; Isaiah saw God in the Temple in the year that King Uzziah died, and the train of his robe filled the Temple; Ezekiel saw visions of God by the river Chebar. But John knows all of this, and that's what makes his apostolic assertation so daring. By the Holy Spirit John asserts that no matter what dreams, visions, revelations, epiphanies, theophanies, or Christophanies people have had in times past, compared to the revelation we have in the Word made flesh, *no one has ever seen God!*

All ideas and images of God must surrender to the supreme revelation of God as seen in Jesus Christ. Christ alone is the perfect definition of who God is. The conclusion we are to draw from John's theopoetics at the beginning of the fourth Gospel is this: God is like Jesus. God has always been like Jesus. There has never been a time when God wasn't like Jesus. We haven't always known this, but now we do.

O God, we thank you that your nature has been revealed to us in your Son, Jesus Christ. And we praise you for the infinite flow of your saving grace that comes to us through your Word made flesh. Amen.

EIGHTH DAY OF CHRISTMAS
JANUARY 1

Luke 2:21
The Holy Name

Happy New Year! Today is both New Year's Day and the eighth day of Christmas because we have two calendars—a secular calendar by which we coordinate time with others and a sacred calendar by which we mark time by telling the story of redemption. On the church calendar, today isn't New Year's Day but Holy Name Day. Jesus, following Jewish tradition, was circumcised and named on his eighth day—or what we call the eighth day of Christmas.

Before Jesus shed blood in his crucifixion, he shed blood in his circumcision. And this blood too is holy. In circumcision Jesus enters the Abrahamic covenant and becomes a true seed of Abraham, *the* true Seed of Abraham. In his mission Jesus becomes Israel embodied as a single person; he takes the vocation of Israel upon his back and carries it through to victory. His vocational mission will be complete when he cries, "It is finished" upon the cross. But he enters his vocational mission when he is circumcised on the eighth day, just like every Jewish male before him

With his circumcision, Mary's firstborn son is given his name: Jesus. This is the name that was given to her by the angel Gabriel at the Annunciation. Jesus, or *Y'shua*, is essentially the same name as Joshua in the Old Testament—a name that means *Yahweh is salvation*. Of course this must be the name of Messiah, for Messiah is the one sent by God to bring salvation. The salvation that comes to us from God is both particular and universal— particular in that it comes by the particular person named Jesus, and universal because it is salvation for the whole world. Regarding particularity the apostle Peter says,

> There is salvation in no one else, for there is no other name under heaven given among men by which we must be saved. (Acts 4:12)

Regarding universality the apostle Paul says,

Therefore God has highly exalted him
and given him the name that is above
    every name,
that at the name of Jesus every knee
    should bow,
in heaven and on earth and under the
    earth,
and every tongue confess
that Jesus Christ is Lord,
to the glory of God the Father.
    (Philippians 2:9–11)

When we speak the name of Jesus, we speak the name of God's salvation. When we believe in the name of Jesus, we believe in the salvation of God. When we call upon the name of Jesus, we call upon the salvation of God. So whether we speak it as Jesus in English or *Y'shua* in Hebrew or *Iesous* in Greek or *Jezui* in Albanian or *Iisus* in Russian or *Gesa* in Italian or *Yesu* in Korean, in this holy name we name our salvation.

On this Holy Name Day, this first day of a new year, I invite you to sit quietly in prayer and speak the name of Jesus over your life, over your family, over the things that trouble you, over the coming year, and to believe that in the name of Jesus the salvation of God shall be seen.

Lord Jesus, your name is salvation, and we call upon your holy name to deliver us from sin, satan, and death, and to grant us admission into the kingdom of your Father. Amen.

NINTH DAY OF CHRISTMAS

JANUARY 2

Matthew 2:1–12
The Magi

Today, tomorrow, and again on Epiphany we will look at the Magi—the wisemen from the East who came to worship the Christ child. The Magi were probably Zoroastrian astronomers and astrologers from Persia who somehow discerned an auspicious sign in the stars that led them on a thousand-mile journey to pay homage to the child born King of the Jews. My favorite commentary on the wisemen is T.S. Eliot's poem *Journey of the Magi.*

Journey of the Magi is written in three stanzas that touch on the difficult journey, the discovery they made, and the distant memory of it all. The poem begins with the demanding expedition in the dead of winter—the stubborn camels and surly camel-drivers, the unfriendly towns and dirty inns charging high prices—the Magi clearly missed their accustomed Persian luxuries. Eventually they arrive at their destination and suddenly it's spring—a lovely prophetic metaphor. This stanza is filled with symbols hinting at the life and death of Jesus— a running stream, a water mill beating the darkness, three trees on the low sky, pieces of silver, and empty wineskins. At last they find the place and are satisfied. Eliot doesn't tell the story of the Magi worshiping Christ—he knows we've heard it.

But what makes this poem so powerful is the third stanza. An old Magi remembers...

All this was a long time ago, I remember,
And I would do it again, but set down
This set down
This: were we led all that way for
Birth or Death? There was a Birth,
    certainly,
We had evidence and no doubt. I had
    seen birth and death,
But had thought they were different; this
    Birth was
Hard and bitter agony for us, like Death,
    our death.

We returned to our palaces, these
    Kingdoms,
But no longer at ease here, in the old
    dispensation,
With an alien people clutching their
    gods.

What T.S. Eliot correctly understands and shows us in his brilliant poem is that with the birth of Christ a new world was born…and an old world died. The old Magi who has seen Christ now describes his own nation as an alien people. From now on the Magi will live in unease as a stranger in his old kingdom. The price of being born anew is dying to the old—this is true for the Magi, for Nicodemus, for me, for you. Being born again is not just a new life, it's also a death. The poem ends with this line:

I should be glad of another death.

What does the Magi mean by this? Is he speaking of his own death? The death of idolatry? Another spiritual death that will lead to a new spiritual rebirth? These are questions worth pondering. Today I encourage you to read T.S. Eliot's poem (you can find it online) and see how it might speak to you.

O God, once we have seen Christ and know him to be the King of Kings, we can never go back to our old lives and old ways. May we ever be on the pilgrim journey that leads us out of idolatry and into your eternal kingdom. Amen.

TENTH DAY OF CHRISTMAS

JANUARY 3

Matthew 2:11

Gold, Frankincense, and Myrrh

When the Magi, guided by a mysterious star and with some help from Jewish scribes who knew Micah's prophecy, finally found the child they sought in Bethlehem, they knelt in worship and presented their now famous gifts. In popular tradition the wisemen are depicted as three in number, but the text doesn't tell us that. The number three comes from the three kinds of gifts—gold, frankincense, and myrrh. Today the trio of gold, frankincense, and myrrh conjures the Christmas ethos as readily as anything else. And hidden in these three gifts are three prophetic witnesses to the identity and mission of the child so diligently sought by the Magi.

Gold has always been a gift fit for a king. When the Queen of Sheba paid her visit to King Solomon she brought a lavish gift of gold. Now these magi, as "kings" of the East, bring a present of gold to the child declared in the stars to be the King of the Jews. The tiny babe in Mary's arms has been born King of the Jews—not *made* King of the Jews like Herod but *born* King of the Jews from the royal line of David. The gift of gold reveals the realpolitik of Christmas. Tomorrow we will see just how deeply King Herod was threatened by this political claim. In his Christmas song, "Cry of A Tiny Babe," Bruce Cockburn puts it like this:

> The child is born in the fullness of time
> Three wise astrologers take note of the
>   signs
> Come to pay their respects to the fragile
>   little king
> Get pretty close to wrecking everything

The second gift of frankincense is a gift fit for deity. This fragrant incense was burnt in temples around the world in honor of the gods, as it was also burnt in the Jerusalem Temple in honor of the God of Israel. The child before whom the Magi knelt in homage is both a king with a real kingdom and the divine Son of God worthy of worship. Of the babe born in Bethlehem the church has come to confess,

> We believe in one Lord, Jesus Christ,
> the only Son of God,
> eternally begotten of the Father,
> God from God, Light from Light,
> true God from true God,
> begotten, not made,
> of one Being with the Father.

Myrrh is the most mysterious of the three gifts. Myrrh was a costly resinous spice that was used in perfumes and also as a burial spice for royalty. Nicodemus contributed a hundred pounds of myrrh (a kingly fortune!) at the burial of Jesus. A burial spice is indeed a strange gift for a newborn child, but it speaks of our Savior's full humanity. Jesus Christ is Immanuel, God with us—not only with us in birth but also with us in death.

Gold, frankincense, and myrrh are the prophetic gifts that bear witness to the Christ child. Gold for the

King of Kings. Frankincense for the God of Gods. Myrrh for Immanuel who will join us in death that we might join him in resurrection.

Lord Jesus, we worship you like the wisemen of old—we worship you as our King, as our God, and as our brother who redeems us from death. Amen.

ELEVENTH DAY OF CHRISTMAS

JANUARY 4

Matthew 2:16–18

The Massacre of the Innocents

Today we look at the dark side of Christmas in a macabre story you won't find on any Christmas card—King Herod's massacre of the innocents. Two thousand years ago Jesus was born into a world where vicious despots were willing to employ hideous violence to hold on to power—which is to say a world not unlike our own. The lethal violence directed at Jesus, first as an infant and then at the end of his life, accentuates the political nature of the kingdom of heaven. This kingdom does nothing less than radically reimagine how the world should be organized. The kingdom that Jesus Christ brings is not a kingdom restricted to heaven, but a kingdom *for* earth coming *from* heaven. Of course, the principalities and powers always view this heavenly invasion as a challenge to their tyranny. When the Magi inquired, "Where is the child who has been born King of the Jews?", it wasn't long before death squads were sent by Herod in an attempt to eliminate his rival. And what was the inscription Pontius Pilate placed upon the cross indicating the capital crime of Jesus? "Jesus of Nazareth, the King of the Jews."

The kingdom of heaven is nonviolent, but that doesn't mean it won't be opposed with violence by those who seek to shape the world through lethal force. Jesus commented on this after John the Baptist was imprisoned by Herod Antipas: "From the days of John the Baptist until now the kingdom of heaven has suffered violence, and the violent attack it." (Matthew 11:12) The temptation is to try to overcome what we deem as unjust violence with what we call just violence. This is the myth of redemptive violence. In its American iteration, redemptive violence is mythologized by the gunslinger in a white hat who sets all wrongs to right with his trusty six-shooter. But the myth of cowboy justice only serves to keep us imprisoned in the bloody world of retaliatory violence. Jesus calls his disciples to live gently in a brutal world; to follow Jesus is to abandon the myth of redemptive violence; to take up the cross of Christ is to renounce the way of the sword.

The death of the innocent children of Bethlehem is what we today call in Orwellian language "collateral damage." I realize that most American Christians don't want to sully their sentimental version of Christmas with Matthew's disturbing account of King Herod's collateral damage—it too easily reminds us of drone strikes gone awry that end up hitting wedding parties instead of terrorist cells. When contemporary superpowers adopt the tactics of ancient tyrant kings, we need to be honest about the fact that innocent people, including children, will be killed. The dark side of Christmas forces us to ask uncomfortable questions about babies killed by covert operations in the name of "security." We tell ourselves that our security forces are very different from those of King Herod, but Rachel weeps for her children all the same.

O God, today we join Rachel in weeping over all the innocent ones who have suffered at the hands of the mighty, and we pray even more earnestly for your kingdom to come and your will to be done on earth as it is in heaven. Amen.

TWELFTH DAY OF CHRISTMAS

JANUARY 5

Matthew 2:13–15, 19–23
The Return from Egypt

We've now arrived at the last day of Christmas, and on the last day of Christmas we see the Holy Family return to the land of Israel after their flight to Egypt. King Herod died in the spring of 4 BC and Jesus may have been as old as two when the family fled to Egypt, so our Gregorian calendar is a bit off—Jesus was probably born around 6 BC. But these historical trivialities, as interesting as they may be, are not what this story is about. The Holy Family's flight to and return from Egypt is about Jesus assuming the identity of Israel. Israel's experience and vocation are embodied in a single person by the true Seed of Abraham, by the true Son of David. Jesus becomes Israel so that Israel's task to bring Yahweh's salvation to the nations might be fulfilled in him.

In the eighth century BC the Hebrew prophet Hosea wrote a poem describing Israel's history of infidelity and Yahweh's faithful love toward Israel despite their failings. The opening line of the poem says,

> When Israel was a child, I loved him,
> and out of Egypt I called my son.
> (Hosea 11:1)

Hosea is hearkening back to the Exodus—when God called Israel out of Egypt. So when the Holy Family went to Egypt it was like when the family of Jacob went to Egypt. And when the Holy Family departed Egypt, it was their Exodus. In recounting the Holy Family's departure after their sojourn in Egypt, Matthew says, "This was to fulfill what had been spoken by the Lord through the prophet, 'Out of Egypt I have called my son.'" (Matthew 2:15)

This is an excellent example of how the first Christians read their Bible (what we call the Old Testament). Every time they went to the Scriptures it was in search of Christ. Prior to Christ you could not have read Hosea 11:1 and predicted that Messiah would be called out of Egypt—it's not a prophecy in that sense. But after the events of Christ, Matthew can read Hosea 11:1 and see an unanticipated fulfillment in Christ. Matthew is not interested in the "authorial intent" of Hosea, Matthew is interested in reading all the Scriptures as about Christ. This is the apostolic and patristic way of reading the Old Testament.

Like Israel, Messiah went down into Egypt and returned to Israel from Egypt. And as Israel spent forty *years* in the wilderness before entering the promised land, Jesus spent forty *days* in the wilderness before entering his ministry. Jesus is Israel realized in a single person and as such fulfills Israel's mission. Truly, Isaiah prophesied that Israel as Yahweh's Servant would not fail in his task. (See Isaiah 42:1–4) All that God appointed Israel to do is accomplished in Christ. The apostle Paul says it like this: "In Christ every one of God's promises is a 'Yes.'" (2 Corinthians 1:20)

O God, we thank you that Jesus is your eternal "Yes" to all the promises you have made—promises that include the salvation of the nations through your servant Israel. Amen.

EPIPHANY
JANUARY 6

Isaiah 60:1–6
Kings Shall Come

Today is Epiphany, the day we commemorate the revelation (epiphany) of Christ to the Gentiles. The first Gentile worshipers of Christ were the wisemen from the East, so one more time we return to the Persian Magi, but this time we do so by looking into the Old Testament.

Isaiah's "Arise, Shine" poem is about a future glory of Zion—a poetic way of speaking of Jerusalem. When Isaiah wrote his poem Jerusalem was in ruins, but the prophet anticipates a day when the glory of the Lord will be seen in a restored Zion. Isaiah prophecies that in a world enshrouded in pagan idolatry a light will rise and shine from Zion that will draw Gentile nations and kings to its brightness. These kings will come with camel caravans loaded with tribute, including gifts of gold and frankincense. In theological parlance this is known as "the eschatological pilgrimage of the nations" and it signals the beginning of Gentiles abandoning their idols to become worshipers of the God of Israel.

In Isaiah 60 we find most of the elements for Matthew's account of the Magi's pilgrimage to Zion to worship the King of the Jews. In our Christmas carols and cards we often speak of three kings and envision them riding camels—images drawn from Isaiah, not Matthew. But we are correct to speak of kings with their camels coming to worship the Christ child because we are correct to connect Matthew 2 with Isaiah 60. Christians reading Isaiah in the first decades after the death and resurrection of Jesus interpreted all the promises of Israel's glorious future as prophecies about Jesus Christ, and Isaiah was an especially rich treasure trove of these prophecies. They read Isaiah and proclaimed that Jesus is Isaiah's virgin-born Immanuel and Prince of Peace in whose kingdom swords are turned to plowshares, and where the lion lays down with the lamb. They also saw Isaiah's prophecy of Gentile nations coming to worship the God of Israel as fulfilled in Gentile converts to Christ. The early Christian theologians didn't read the eschatological prophecies of Isaiah to find out what will happen in the future, but to discover what has already been accomplished with the coming of Christ.

Isaiah prophecies of how Zion will rise and shine in a dark world and draw Gentile worshipers to the land of Israel. Matthew tells of Magi led to Israel by the rising and shining of a star. Years ago I was fascinated by the star of Bethlehem—I read many books positing various theories about what the star might have been. Today that's not what I'm interested in. For Matthew, the important thing is not how the Magi knew that the King of the Jews had been born, but what their eschatological pilgrimage portended. For Matthew, Gentiles from the East coming to Zion to pay homage to Christ with gifts of gold and frankincense heralded the arrival of all that the Hebrew prophets had foretold. The pilgrimage of the Magi means that in Jesus Christ the savior of the world has appeared.

O God, we praise you for the glory of your salvation that has risen and shines in the world through your Son Jesus Christ. May we, like the Magi, ever rejoice with exceeding great joy. Amen.